The ENDURING PRINCIPLES *of the* AMERICAN FOUNDING

Edited by Matthew Spalding

The Heritage Foundation

Published by The Heritage Foundation
214 Massachusetts Avenue, NE
Washington, DC 20002
800.544.4843
www.heritage.org

Cover design by Woodpile Studios, www.woodpilestudios.com

Copyright © 2001 by The Heritage Foundation
ISBN 0-89195-095-8

"The preservation of the sacred fire of liberty, and the destiny of the republican model of government, are justly considered as *deeply*, perhaps as *finally*, staked on the experiment entrusted to the hands of the American people."

George Washington
First Inaugural Address, April 30, 1789

TABLE OF CONTENTS

INTRODUCTION

———⟫●⟪———

MATTHEW SPALDING

Americans usually refer to the starting point of this nation's history as the American Revolution. The word "revolution" correctly suggests the great change brought about when the united colonies declared and then established their independence from Great Britain in order to form a new nation.

Those who established the United States were indeed revolutionaries, profoundly convinced that they were inaugurating, as it says on the Great Seal printed on the back of every dollar bill, a *novus ordo seclorum*—a new order of the ages. But their new order—unlike the great sociopolitical upheavals of France in 1789 and Russia in 1917, both of which violently overthrew the existing order in the name of radical ideology— did not lead to guillotines and gulags. The revolution in America, though ultimately settled by force of arms, was a deliberative revolution that resulted in the establishment of constitutional government, the rule of law, and ordered liberty.

The first number of *The Federalist Papers*, the great series of essays by Alexander Hamilton, James Madison, and John Jay that advocated the ratification of the United States Constitution, opens dramatically by noting that it seems to have been left to the people of America "to decide the important question whether societies of men are really capable or not of establishing good government from reflection and choice, or whether they are forever destined to depend for their political constitutions on accident and force." The wrong answer to this question—which many leading American statesmen feared—would be to "the great misfortune of mankind."

Earlier, General George Washington, in one of his last addresses as commander in chief of the continental army, had made the equally striking point: "According to the system of policy the states shall adopt at this moment, they will stand or fall; and by their confirmation or lapse, it is yet to be decided, whether the Revolution must ultimately be considered as a blessing or a curse: a blessing or a curse, not to the present age alone, for with our fate will the destiny of unborn millions be involved."

The United States is unique in that it was intentionally brought into being—that is, founded—based upon certain principles held to be true for all mankind. These principles were arrived at by reflection and choice rather than accidental circumstances or the application of force. The leaders of the American Revolution had a decent regard for former times and traditions; they were close students of history. Nevertheless, as James Madison noted in *Federalist* 14, they did not allow "a blind veneration for antiquity, for custom or for names, to overrule the suggestions of their own good common sense, the knowledge of their own situation and the lessons of their own experience." Instead, the American Founders pursued "a new and more noble course" and "accomplished a revolution which has no parallel in the annals of human society." They *"formed the design"* of a new nation.

What were the principles of the American Founding? Consider the definitive American statement of our first principles, the Declaration of Independence: "We hold these Truths to be self-evident, that all Men are created equal, that they are endowed by their Creator with certain unalienable Rights, that among these are Life, Liberty and the Pursuit of Happiness." Because all men by nature equally possess *rights*, government derives its just *powers* from the consent of the governed. The purpose of government is to secure these fundamental rights. And although prudence tells us that governments should not be changed for trivial reasons, the people retain the right to alter or abolish government when it becomes destructive of these ends. It is in light of this statement of principle—laying out the conditions of legitimate political authority, the ends of government, and the sovereignty of the people—that the representatives of the Continental Congress, with "a firm reliance on the Protection of Divine Providence," declared themselves to be free and independent.

The challenge of the Constitutional Convention was to create the institutional arrangements for limiting power and securing the rights promised in the Declaration of Independence while preserving a republican form of government that reflected the consent of the governed. The Framers' solution was to create a strong government of adequate but limited powers, all carefully enumerated in a written constitution. In addition to an energetic executive, a bicameral legislature, and an independent judiciary, its structural arrangements include a system of separated powers—giving each branch different functions and responsibilities so that none dominates—and federalism, which divides authority between the national and state governments.

John Adams declared the three-and-a-half-month Constitutional Convention "the greatest single effort of national deliberation that the world has ever seen." The result was the United States Constitution, today the longest lasting, most successful, most enviable and imitated constitution man has ever known.

But what are the *enduring* principles of the American Founding? One way to answer this question is to consider the American Founding as it has developed over time, looking for the "evolving" themes of our "living" Constitution in order to determine the progressive ideas of our democracy. This approach is especially popular among today's academic elites, for whom everything changes and adapts to accommodate modern culture. A better way would be to determine what the Founders themselves thought were the most important principles of the Founding, why they understood those principles to be necessary for the success of free government, and then consider how those principles have managed since. This is what we asked some of America's most prominent thinkers to do, looking particularly at how those principles have fared over the course of the twentieth century. The essays in this volume are their considered answers.

In his essay, Edwin J. Feulner suggests that a good starting point is to remind ourselves what the American Founders meant by various terms—he begins by considering what they meant by self-evident truths and popular sovereignty—that are hotly debated today. He points out that to be rightly understood we must first be rightly informed (that is, educated) about what the Founders meant in the first place. This goes for elected representatives as well. The people should "trust their representatives to govern well," Feulner concludes, but "a large part of restoring that trust is returning government authority to its proper—that is, constitutional—scope."

Michael Novak writes about the axioms of liberty and how they are insufficient without the religious faith that was always understood—and should be recalled today—as indispensable to free government. For some time, scholars have stressed the principles of the American Founding that come from John Locke and the Enlightenment, but Novak tells six stories to illustrate the religious principles from Judaism and Christianity (especially Judaism) that inform America. "It is important for citizens today," he writes, "whose main inspiration is the Enlightenment and Reason to grasp the religious elements in the Founding, which have been understated for a hundred years."

Kim Holmes and Malcolm Wallop consider the Founders' enduring principles as they apply to the realm of foreign policy and world affairs. While both seek to define a prudent course informed by those principles, Holmes emphasizes the relationship between interest and character and suggests how important it is that our international policies be guided by our national character. "It is true that America is the beacon and hope for the entire world," he writes, "but in order for it to shine abroad, it must first be burning bright at home." Wallop discusses the original themes of our foreign policy, stressing independence, national unity, and love of country, and illustrates how these principles informed us from the beginning, through the crisis of Civil War and into the early twentieth century. "In this century, however, even as our statesmen have de-emphasized our differences from the rest of the world, or even deprecated the inflexibility of American morals," Wallop warns, "American foreign policy has been characterized by ideas and practices that violate the timeless norms of statecraft."

Walter Williams and Charles Kesler are both concerned about the principles of constitutional government and how these principles can be revived. Williams emphasizes the restraints placed on government power from the beginning and argues that we need to relearn what the Constitution does and does not permit. "Tragically," he writes, "today's Americans are running away from the ideals of the American Revolution at a breakneck speed." Kesler, for his part, wonders whether we still live in the same republic as the one constituted in 1787. His essay traces the rise of a new theory of constitutional government that developed in the twentieth century—starting with the Progressive Movement and then the rise of modern liberalism—to challenge the older order established by the American Founders. "We need three branches of government that are interested in restoring constitutionalism," he writes, "and to get that we need political parties that are willing to take a stand on behalf of the original Constitution and against the new Constitution of the Second Republic."

In his essay, Robert Bork wonders whether the American Founders would be happy with America today. The answer, not surprisingly, is yes and no. On the one hand, he is greatly concerned about what he calls a "therapeutic heresy" caused by an overwhelmingly secular intellectual class and the collapse of popular mores that came with the cultural revolution in the 1960s. "With the decline in civic virtue and politicization of the universities, necessarily came a weakening of Americans' attachments to legitimate governmental processes," he observes, "and with that self-restraint, which values the preservation of democratic procedures over immediate gratification of one's desires." Yet this famous pessimist does not conclude that all is lost—he sees discernible and strong countertrends. "There are no Ronald Reagans to be seen in our politics today and chances are there will never be another," concludes Bork, "but that means instead of waiting for a savior, we will have to work harder to achieve our own and America's salvation."

One last question: Can this nation, or any nation so conceived, long *endure*? The question that Abraham Lincoln asked at Gettysburg—when he reminded us that we are a nation conceived in liberty and dedicated to the proposition that all men are created equal—still stands, unanswered definitively. Indeed, it looms large over each of the essays in this collection. The dilemma, both then and now, is that the permanence of America's principles does not necessarily mean that the nation dedicated to them will last quite as long. This is because the principles of liberty and self-government—as opposed, say, to the dictates of communism or socialism—have to be taught over and over again to each new generation of citizens. "If a nation expects to be ignorant and free in a state of civilization," Thomas Jefferson once warned, "it expects what never was and never will be."

The Founders knew that the Constitution and the institutional arrangements they carefully designed were crucially important for the success of the new republic. But in the end, they knew that good citizens—who know their rights as well as their responsibilities—were necessary for the survival of republican government. This is why the American Founders constantly reminded themselves and their posterity that the great nation they created was, and always by its nature would remain, an experiment. "The preservation of the sacred fire of liberty, and the destiny of the republican model of government," Washington powerfully remarked in his First Inaugural, "are justly considered as deeply, perhaps as finally, staked on the experiment entrusted to the hands of the American people."

As we approach the two hundred and twenty-fifth anniversary of our independence, it remains the case that the only way to make the principles of the American Founding truly enduring is to revive and enliven them in the hearts and minds of the American people. This was as true at the end of the eighteenth century as it is today at the beginning of the twenty-first. Our generation's success at this never-ending task, thus far so nobly advanced, will decide for our time—and significantly determine for the future—the important question of whether government of the people, by the people, and for the people shall or shall not perish from the Earth.

THE STATE OF THE FOUNDING PRINCIPLES

<hr/>

EDWIN J. FEULNER

Welcome to The Heritage Foundation's Annual Board Meeting and Public Policy Seminar. We open two days of sessions built around the theme of "The Enduring Principles of the American Founding." A glance at the speakers on the agenda will tell you that when the sessions end, all of us will have a better understanding of our nation's founding principles.

Perhaps that theme, "The Enduring Principles of the American Founding," should be taken more as a question than a statement. Much of this weekend will be devoted to addressing, directly or indirectly, such questions as:

- Which of our founding principles have endured?
- Which have not endured, and what has happened to them?
- How do we restore lost principles?

I'll break the ice this morning by raising a few such questions, and to get at those questions I want to focus on two principles that the Founders clearly accepted.

The first is the idea of self-evident truths. All of us know those famous words from the Declaration: "We hold these truths to be self-evident...." Yet, in today's roiling policy battles, it often appears that everything is open to debate and nothing is self-evident. So I will explore this puzzling state of affairs, and in that context I'll tell you how our work at The Heritage Foundation is guided by the Founders' conviction that the most fundamental truths are self-evident.

The second principle from the founding I will discuss is one you will recognize as one of Ronald Reagan's favorite maxims: Trust the people. The American Founders not only trusted the people, they built that trust into a system of government, the likes of which had never been seen before. But they also qualified that trust, and on that point I will conclude with some questions that should be thought-provoking for conservatives.

As a bonus, I will show you that life is fair, prayers are answered, and dreams come true—I will do all that in less than 30 minutes.

So let me turn directly to the principle of self-evident truths. In the Declaration, the Founders stated several propositions they held to be self-evidently true: all men are created equal and are equally endowed with the inalienable rights to life, liberty, and the pursuit of happiness.

Today, if there's universal agreement that all men are equal, there is not universal agreement about the definition of equality. Conservatives define equality by the *opportunity* to pursue happiness, while liberals define it by the *outcomes* of the pursuit. This dispute is, of course, famous and endless.

Although the Founders mentioned the inalienable rights of life, liberty, and the pursuit of happiness as self-evident truths, they plainly left room for other such truths in their phrase "among these" truths.

It is helpful to think what some of those other truths might be. Despite our seemingly endless disagreements with the left, we do agree on a number of important propositions that seem to be self-evidently true. For instance, we agree:

- That a well-educated child is better off than a poorly educated child.
- That a person who earns a living is better off than one who must depend on others.
- That neighbors who are neighborly and trusting toward one another are better off than neighbors who don't know and don't trust one another, and so on.

But, here again, beneath such agreement lies seemingly intractable disagreement. If we agree that a child needs a good education, we disagree about how to deliver it. Progressives have one answer, traditionalists another. Advocates of whole language stand off against advocates of phonics. Rote learning of important facts clashes with the self-directed "discovery" approach to learning.

If we agree that self-reliant adults are better off than dependent adults, we disagree about how to nurture self-reliance. The welfare reforms of 1996, which center on personal responsibility and conditional beneficence, touched off storms of disagreement. And despite the manifest success of those reforms, the disagreements are still rumbling.

Is there any hope of making progress in such debates? I think so, and the place to begin is with a better understanding of how America's Founding Fathers viewed the idea of self-evident truth. One of the philosophers who greatly influenced Jefferson, and many of his contemporaries, was Thomas Reid, the Scottish philosopher of common sense.

From his study of Reid, Jefferson understood that the apprehension of self-evident truth doesn't necessarily come easily or automatically. Reid wrote a great deal about this. He said that any ordinary person can grasp self-evident truths if they are distinctly set before him, and if he "takes due pains to be rightly informed."

Now I would suggest that taking pains to be rightly informed need not be restricted to the informed; the informers can also take such pains. And at Heritage we are very much in the business of taking pains to rightly inform people about policies by setting the issues *distinctly before them*, to use Thomas Reid's phrase.

One way we do this is through the highly technical field of data analysis. About five years ago, we began building what has since become our Center for Data Analysis. During our 25th anniversary campaign over the past two years, we directed more resources toward this work and developed some exciting new ways to quantitatively forecast the effects of changes in tax and other social policies at the individual and family level.

Let me give you an example of how this work pays off. Congress has been debating a proposal to reduce the bizarre tax known as the marriage penalty. This policy says that if a man and woman live together out of wedlock, they pay a certain tax rate. If they get married, their tax burden instantly increases.

In February, CDA produced a study that shows by congressional district how many married couples in each district are penalized by this strange tax. Incidentally, this simple list required us to solve some truly groundbreaking mathematical problems because the federal data isn't sorted by congressional district. But it was worth the effort, because last month during House debate of the proposed reforms, Members cited Heritage numbers no fewer than 60 times in one session. Forty-four different Members, including Speaker Hastert and seven Democrats, used our data, and the full spreadsheet from our study was entered in the *Congressional Record*.

Just as important, newspapers around the country carried stories about the effect of the marriage penalty in their communities—thanks to our public-relations efforts. In the end, the House passed the bill overwhelmingly, with 48 Democrats joining the majority. At least 30 of those Democrats said that our research and the media coverage back home made a difference.

That is an example of the payoff when we sweat the details and set issues clearly and distinctly before Congress and the American people. As we continue to refine our forecasting models, we will be able to plug in a growing range of social policy reforms and give rough but credible *quantitative* answers to questions like the following. If a certain policy reform is implemented,

- How many more, or fewer, marriages are likely to end in divorce?

- How much more, or less, will families be able to save?

- How many more, or fewer, children will be able to attend college?

- How many more, or fewer, families will be able to own a home?

- How many more, or fewer, people will be able to afford health insurance?

What I want to emphasize is that this work is directly related to the way the Founders understood the idea of self-evident truth. As I said earlier, all of us—left or right—regard it as self-evident that well-educated children are better off than poorly educated children, and so on.

And though we often disagree about the means of achieving such self-evident goods, those disagreements are not doomed to be endless. In many cases they can be resolved by the sorts of quantitative measures I just mentioned, measures we are learning to generate at Heritage. In relatively uncontroversial terms, these studies set issues *distinctly before* the people who must decide them. Now, we all know that conservative policy-makers haven't distinguished themselves in the past few years. But they aren't the only people who make public policy. That job is shared by the people—as in "We the people of the United States." That is why we've expanded our efforts at Heritage to better educate the general public by creating our Center for Media and Public Policy. If we set the issues distinctly before them, if we take pains to rightly inform them in the ways I described, they will understand the kinds of self-evident goods I mentioned earlier. Toward that end, we are working on a number of priorities this year.

- We support a tax system that would promote prosperity for all by making taxes simpler, lower, and fairer.
- We support a missile defense system because the first obligation of government is to protect the American people against foreign aggression.
- We support personalized Social Security accounts to give all Americans the opportunity to save for their

own retirement rather than depend on the whims of future politicians.

- We support school choice because we want America to have the best schools in the world, so our children will have the education and opportunity to succeed.

- Because all Americans should be free to choose their own health care providers, we favor reforms to increase competition and lower costs.

- Because too many government programs actually hurt their intended beneficiaries, we encourage non-government solutions to local problems as the essence of civil society.

By developing such resources as our Center for Data Analysis, we are increasingly learning how to set the truth about these issues emphatically before the American people. And this strategy rests on the second principle of the Founders I want to talk about: Trust the people.

If we want to know how the Founders understood that principle, the place to begin is with the question: Trust the people to do *what*? Because the Founders were republicans with a small "R," and not democrats with a small "D," their answer to this was clear: The people can be and should be entrusted with deciding who will govern. "Trust the people" as the Founders understood it meant: Trust the people to do some things—but not *all* things.

In his Heritage 25 Lecture on Leadership in January 1999, George Will noted that the Founders deliberately created a "constitutional distance" between elected representatives and the people. Let me quote a few lines from his lecture:

> The original idea of the republic ... was representation, and the point of representation is that the people do not decide issues; they decide who will

decide. In a republic, the question is not whether the elite shall rule; it is *which* elite shall rule, and the task of governments is to get consent to good government.

Taking this notion of a republic seriously, the Founders and their successors seldom sought the public's ear and took little interest in molding public opinion. As Will noted in his lecture, George Washington gave an average of only three speeches a year during his presidency. John Adams gave one. Jefferson was a relatively big talker with five speeches a year.

Andrew Jackson spoke publicly about once a year. But his populist views gave birth to Jacksonian democracy and supplied an ideological lever for narrowing the constitutional distance the Founders put between the people and their representatives. In his annual message to Congress delivered in December 1833, Jackson took up the question—one of his favorite hobby horses—of whether government deposits were safe in the Bank of the United States. Here is what he said to Members of the House and Senate:

> Coming as you do, for the most part, immediately from the people and the states by election, and possessing the fullest opportunity to know their sentiments, the present Congress will be sincerely solicitous to carry into full and fair effect the will of their constituents in regard to this institution.

So, under the lens of Jacksonian democracy, "Trust the people" means "Know the people's sentiments and be sincerely solicitous to put them into effect." And that is quite different from how the Founders understood the republic that they established.

Now, we can bring this topic up to the present day by solving the following riddle: What do you get if you put Jacksonian democracy on steroids and add jet air travel, nationwide television, telephones, fax machines, and the Internet—and then place all of that at the disposal of elected officials who take their compass bearings not from the North Pole but from the Gallup Poll?

You get "Clintonian" democracy. You get a federal government that knows nothing of a constitutional distance between itself and the people. It knows only a continuous, cloying, and morbid contact with the people. This is *not* what Ronald Reagan meant when he said "Trust the people," and it certainly wasn't what the Founders had in mind for the republic when they placed a constitutional distance between the government and the people.

When I began, I said I would conclude with some questions that should be thought-provoking for conservatives. So let me put the general question this way: As conservatives, we are republicans with a small "R" and Jeffersonian democrats with a small "D." Yet we are living at time when representative government operates as a Jacksonian enterprise. Elected representatives are nothing if not solicitous of voters' sentiments on every imaginable issue. And voters generally see their elected representatives as agents to carry out their will on specific issues.

If voters want to tune in on what Congress is up to, they have the technology for doing so at their fingertips. They can dial up C-SPAN and see their representatives at the podium. Through the Internet, they can read bills, committee reports, floor debates, and anything else on the public record. If they fire off an e-mail, it arrives in their representative's computer about 10 seconds later.

Conversely, if Members of Congress want to know what's on their constituents' minds, an almost daily stream of scientific opinion polls will tell them. If they want to manipulate public opinion, they can use all the latest communications technologies to bombard their constituents with their spin on any given issue—and then poll to see what effect the spin might have had.

We cannot step outside this system and operate in a vacuum. We have to play the hand we are dealt. We have to work within the prevailing framework, and that framework is—for now—Jacksonian. The example I described a moment ago about the marriage penalty was a policy victory we won by playing according to the Jacksonian rules of the game—by setting that issue clearly before the Congress and the constituents they aim to please.

So, the question is: Are we all Jacksonians now? Or can we work within today's Jacksonian framework to restore the Founders' Jeffersonian principles and re-open a constitutional distance between the people and their representatives? The question may seem a bit disconcerting. But, as you well know, I never got out of the pessimistic side of a bed in my life, and this morning—back here where I studied 35 years ago—was no exception. So let me suggest in broad terms how I think we should approach this puzzle.

First, we should recognize that although communications technologies are a conspicuous *part* of the problem, they aren't the *primary* part. To see what I mean, consider this analogy: Any of us could use communications technologies to keep in daily touch with the managers of mutual funds in which we've invested. We could endlessly badger them to manage the funds according to our individual wishes. And they, if they chose, could be solicitous Jacksonians and constantly poll our opinions and curry favor with the dominant factions. That is, they could act like Members of Congress.

But, in fact, the vast empire of mutual funds doesn't work that way, even though millions of Americans have entrusted large chunks of their life savings to fund managers. The world of mutual funds is largely a Jeffersonian enterprise that spontaneously maintains a "constitutional distance" between fund managers and individual investors.

What this shows us is that important institutions of national scope—institutions in which the people have enormous financial stakes—can and do operate on Jeffersonian principles. Institutions of investment and institutions of government have access to the same communications technologies. Yet the former are Jeffersonian and the latter are Jacksonian.

But why is this? In a nutshell, I stated the answer a moment ago: People *entrust* their money to fund mangers. But they do not *entrust* government to their elected representatives. Ironically, this is borne out by the polls that the politicians live by. In the 1950s, about 70 percent of Americans said they trusted the federal government to do the right thing most of the time. Today, only about 30 percent express such trust. Today, despite vastly improved communications between the people and their government, we do not have better government or greater trust. We have precisely the contrary.

So, to give a short answer to a large question, I think the Founders' constitutional distance will begin to re-open when more people begin to trust their representatives to govern well. And a large part of restoring that trust is returning government authority to its proper—that is, constitutional—scope.

This is something we can accomplish one step at a time within today's Jacksonian framework. That is essentially what our scores of programs at Heritage aim to do. Whatever the particular issue—whether it's the marriage penalty, the death tax, over-reaching regulation, welfare policy, national defense, or rebuilding the institutions of civil society—we are on a principled course toward two broad objectives:

- First, government must stop doing things the Founding Fathers never meant for it to do, and

- Second, government must do a better job at those things it was established to do.

For either objective, God is in the details. At Heritage we are taking pains to rightly inform both the Congress and the people about issues of governing. By leaps and bounds, we are developing new ways to set controversial issues distinctly before these groups. I've described a few examples this morning, and we describe a host of others in our just-released Annual Report.

Right now, Heritage can do this better than any other organization—conservative or liberal—in America. We achieved that capability because we understand that the new technologies are not dark forces destined to crowd out the Founding principles; they are powerful tools that, when intelligently used, can help restore those principles to their intended place in American life.

As we look ahead, what course should we set at Heritage? I think the best answer is expressed by another prescription we heard from Ronald Reagan when America was making incremental gains on large problems: Stay the course.

SACRED HONOR:
RELIGIOUS PRINCIPLE IN THE
AMERICAN FOUNDING

————⟫●⟪————

MICHAEL NOVAK

Our preoccupation is a serious one because we're no longer certain of the future. How long are we going to keep this experiment, this America? We are "testing whether this nation can long endure," Lincoln said at Gettysburg. We're still testing. Does the century about to begin mark our last? Is America a meteor that blazed across the heavens and is now exhausted? Or rather is our present moral fog a transient time of trial, those hours cold and dark before the ramparts new gleaming? Are we near our end or at a beginning?

In answer to these questions, I want to tell six brief stories to illustrate the religious principles of the American founding. For a hundred years scholars have stressed the principles that come from the Enlightenment and from Locke in particular. But there are also first principles that come to us from Judaism and Christianity, especially from Judaism. Indeed, it is important to recognize that most of what our Founders talked about (when they talked politically) came from the Jewish Testament, not the Christian. The Protestant Christians who led the way in establishing the principles of this country were uncommonly attached to the Jewish Testament.

Scholars often mistakenly refer to the god of the Founders as a deist god. But the Founders talked about God in terms that are radically Jewish: Creator, Lawgiver, Governor, Judge, and Providence. These were the names they most commonly used for Him, notably in the Declaration. For the most part, these are not names that could have come from the Greeks or Romans, but only from the Jewish Testament. Perhaps the Founders avoided Christian language because they didn't want to divide one another, since different colonies were founded under different Christian inspirations. In any case all found common language in the language of the Jewish Testament. It is important for citizens today whose main inspiration is the Enlightenment and Reason to grasp the religious elements in the founding, which have been understated for a hundred years.

These principles are important to many fellow citizens, and they are indispensable to the moral health of the Republic, as Washington taught us in his Farewell Address: "Of all the dispositions and habits which lead to political prosperity, religion and morality are indispensable supports."

Reason and faith are the two wings by which the American eagle took flight.

If tonight I stress the second wing, the Jewish especially, it is because scholars have paid too much attention to Jefferson in these matters and ignored the other one hundred top Founders. For instance, we've ignored John Witherspoon, the president of Princeton, "the most influential professor in the history of America," who taught one president (Madison stayed an extra year at Princeton to study with him), a vice president, three Supreme Court justices including the chief justice, 12 members of the Continental Congress, 5 delegates to the Constitutional Convention, 14 members of the State Conventions (that ratified the Constitution). During the revolution, many of his pupils were in positions of command in the American forces. We've ignored Dr. Benjamin Rush of Pennsylvania, John Wilson of Pennsylvania, and a host of others.

Tonight I want to quote from some of the Founders to give you a taste of the religious energy behind the founding. Here is my first little story:

> President Jefferson was on his way to church on a Sunday morning with his large red prayer book under his arm [I'm reading from a diary of a minister of that time] when a friend querying him after their mutual good morning said, "Which way are you walking Mr. Jefferson?" [You have to understand that in those days, in Jefferson's administration, the largest church service was in the United States Congress, and, later, the second largest was in the Supreme Court building.] To which he replied, "To Church, Sir." "You going to church Mr. J? You do not believe a word in it." "Sir," said Mr. J. "No nation has ever yet existed or been governed without religion. Nor can be. The Christian religion is the best religion that has ever been given to man and I as chief Magistrate of this nation am bound to give it the sanction of my example. Good morning, Sir."

Note what Jefferson is saying. He didn't say he believed in the Christian God; he evaded that point. But Jefferson did agree with what all his colleagues in the founding thought, that a people cannot maintain liberty without religion. Here is John Adams, 1776:

I sometimes tremble to think that although we are engaged in the best cause that ever employed the human heart, yet the prospect of success is doubtful, not for want of power or of wisdom but of virtue.

The founding generation had no munitions factory this side of the ocean, and yet they were facing the most powerful army and the largest navy in the world. Besides, their unity was fragile. The people of Virginia did not like the people of Massachusetts. The people of Massachusetts did not think highly of the people of Georgia. Reflecting on this point, President Witherspoon, who had just arrived from Scotland in 1768 and was not at first in favor of it, gave a famous sermon in April 1776 supporting independence two months before July 4. His text was read in all 500 Presbyterian churches in the colonies and widely reproduced. Witherspoon argued that although hostilities had been going on for two years, the king still did not understand that he could easily have divided the colonies and ended the hostilities. That the king didn't do so showed that he was not close enough to know how to govern the Americans.

If they were to stick together with people they didn't particularly like, the Americans needed virtues of tolerance, civic spirit, and a love of the common good. Further, because the new nation couldn't compete in armed power, the colonists depended on high moral qualities in their leaders and on devotion in the people. In order to win, for instance, Washington had to avoid frontal combat, and to rely on the moral endurance of his countrymen year after year. To this end, Washington issued an order that any soldier who used profane language would be drummed out of the army. He impressed upon his men that they were fighting for a cause that demanded a special moral appeal, and he wanted no citizen to be shocked by the language and behavior of his troops. The men must show day-by-day that they fought under a special moral covenant.

Now think of our predicament today. How many people in America today can understand the four key words that once formed a great mosaic over the American Republic? *Truth*, we "hold these truths"; *Liberty,* "conceived in liberty"; *Law,* "liberty under law"; and *Judge,* "appealing to the Supreme Judge of the world for the rectitude of our intentions." On the face of things, our Founders were committing treason. In the eyes of the world, they were seditious. They appealed to an objective world, and beyond the eyes of an objective world, they appealed to the Supreme Judge for the rectitude of their intentions. That great mosaic, which used to form the beautiful, colorful apse over the American Republic, in this nonjudgmental age has fallen to the dust. It is disassembled in a thousand pieces. Fewer every year remember how it used to look.

A Second Story. In the first days of September 1774, from every region, members of the First Continental Congress were riding dustily toward Philadelphia, where they hoped to remind King George III of the rights due to them as Englishmen. That's all they were claiming, the rights of Englishmen. And they wanted to remind King George that they were wards of the king. They weren't founded by the Parliament, they were founded by the king, and they resented the Parliament taxing them. The Parliament had nothing to do with their relationship to the king, they thought. Yet, as these delegates were gathering, news arrived that the king's troops were shelling Charlestown and Boston, and rumors flew that the city was being sacked, and robbery and murder were being committed. Those rumors turned out not to be true, but that's the news they heard. Thus, as they gathered, the delegates were confronted with impending war. Their first act as a Continental Congress was to request a session of prayer.

Mr. Jay of New York and Mr. Rutledge of South Carolina immediately spoke against this motion. They said that Americans are so divided in religious sentiments, some Episcopalians, some Quakers, some Anabaptists, some Presbyterians, and some Congregationalists, all could not join in the same act of prayer. Sam Adams rose to say he's no bigot, and could hear a prayer from any gentleman of piety and virtue as long as he is a patriot. "I've heard of a certain Reverend Duché," he said, speaking of the rector of Christ Church down the street from where they were meeting. "People say he's earned that character." Adams moved that the same be asked to read prayers before Congress on the next morning. And the motion carried.

Thus it happened that the first act of the Congress on September 7, 1774, was an official prayer, pronounced by an Episcopalian clergyman dressed in his pontificals. And what did he read? He read a Jewish prayer, Psalm 35 in the Book of Common Prayer. Now imagine the king's troops moving against the homes of some of the people gathered there. Imagine the delegates from South Carolina and New York thinking that the fleet might be shelling their homes soon.

> Plead my cause, O Lord, with them that strive with me. Fight against them that fight against me. Take hold of buckler and shield, and rise up for my help. Say to my soul, "I am your salvation." Let those be ashamed and dishonored who seek my life. Let those be turned back and humiliated who devise evil against me.

Before the Reverend Duché knelt Washington, Henry, Randolph, Rutledge, Lee, and Jay; and by their side, with heads bowed, the Puritan patriots who could imagine at that moment that their own homes being bombarded and overrun. Over these bowed heads the Reverend Duché uttered what all testified was an eloquent prayer for America, for Congress, for the Province of Massachusetts Bay, and especially for the town of Boston. The emotion in the room was palpable, and John Adams wrote to Abigail that night that he had never heard a better prayer or one so well pronounced. "I never saw a greater effect upon an audience. It seemed as if heaven had ordained that that Psalm be read on that morning. It was enough to melt a stone. I saw tears gush into the eyes of the old, grave pacific Quakers of Philadelphia. I must beg you, Abigail, to read that Psalm."

In this fashion, right at its beginning, this nation formed a covenant with God which is repeated in the Declaration: "with a firm reliance on the protection of Divine Providence." The Founders pledged their fidelity to the will of God, and asked God to protect their liberty. They further enacted this covenant in many later acts of Congress regarding Days of Fasting. Within the first six months, for instance, Congress put out a proclamation that every American state set aside a day of prayer and fasting:

> December 11, 1776: *Resolved* that it be recommended to all the United States as soon as possible to appoint a day of solemn fasting and humiliation to implore the Almighty God to forgiveness of the many sins prevailing among all ranks and to beg the countenance and the assistance of his Providence in the prosecution of the present just and necessary war.

And then, within another year, an act of Congress instituted a Day of Thanksgiving to commemorate the signal successes of that year, and again the next year. Years later, in *The Federalist* No. 38, Publius marveled at the improbable unanimity achieved among fragmented delegates, from free states and slave, from small states and large, from rich states and poor. "It is impossible for the man of pious reflection not to perceive in it a finger of the Almighty hand which has been so frequently and signally extended to our relief in the critical stages of the revolution." Three times *The Federalist* notes the blessings of Providence upon this country.

A Third Story. On the night before the battle of Long Island, the Americans received intelligence that the British were attacking the next morning, and Washington was trapped with his whole army. Washington saw that there was only one way out—by boat. During the night, the Americans gathered as many boats as they could. There weren't enough. Morning came, and more than half the army was still on shore. A huge fog rolled in and covered them till noon. They escaped, and when the British closed the trap, there was no one there. The Americans interpreted that fog as an act of Providence.

In the preaching of the time, Americans learned as follows: Providence does not mean that God works magically; rather, from all time every detail of the tapestry is known to the one who weaves it. To the Eternal God, there is neither time nor sequence, but every detail of the tapestry is visible to Him as if in one simultaneous moment, each thing acting independently and freely, but cohering as a whole, like characters in a well-wrought novel. Thus, the rival general, on the morning of the great battle comes down with dysentery and can't concentrate. Nothing more common in the affairs of human beings than circumstance and chance, which only those who lived through them in time and sequence found to be surprising. The very sermon Witherspoon preached on behalf of independence in April 1776 was a sermon on how Providence acts by contingent and indirect actions—not *foreseen*, because God doesn't "foresee" anything. He's *present* to everything, in the Jewish and Christian understanding. He's not *before* or *after*, He's present to all things at one time. And like a great novelist, He sees the details of what He does, and how they all hook together, without forcing anybody's liberty, without manipulating anything.

A Fourth Story. When Jefferson wrote the Declaration of Independence, he mentioned God twice. Before the Congress would sign it, members insisted on two more references to God. Thus, the four names already mentioned: the *Author* of nature and nature's laws; the *Creator* who endowed in us our rights; the *Judge* to whom we appeal in witness that our motives spring not out of seditiousness, but from a dear love of liberty, and a deep sense of our own proper dignity; and a trust in *Divine Providence.*

The fundamental meaning of the Jewish, and later the Christian, Bible is that the axis of the universe is what happens in the interior of the human being. Every story in the Bible is a story of what happens in the arena of the human will. In one chapter King David is faithful to his Lord and in the next, not. And the suspense of every chapter is, What will humans choose next? Liberty is the reason God made the universe. He wanted somewhere one creature capable of recognizing that He had made all things, that the creation is good, and that He had extended his hand in friendship. He wanted at least one creature to be able, not as a slave but as a free woman or a free man, to reciprocate his proffered friendship. That, in a nutshell, is what Judaism is, and what Christianity is. (Christianity, of course, played an historical role in making the God of Judaism known universally.)

The members of Congress on July 2, 1776, were about to make themselves liable to the charge of treason and to humiliate their children into the *n*th generation for being the descendants of traitors. They needed that reference to their *Judge* in the Declaration. And they wanted that reference to *Providence,* to declare that God is on the side of Liberty, and those who trust in liberty will therefore prevail. Whatever the odds, Providence will see to it that they prevail.

Let me recall, from one of the old American hymns, words that reflect exactly this biblical vision. This world didn't just "happen," it was created. It was created for a purpose, and that purpose is *liberty:*

> Our fathers God! To Thee,
> Author of liberty,
> To Thee we sing.
> Long may our land be bright
> With freedom's holy light;
> Protect us by Thy might,
> Great God our king.

A typical sentiment of the American people then, and even now.

I've mentioned that though some historians say they were deists, the early Americans who believed that the lifting of the fog on Long Island was an act of God, were not deists. Their god was not a "watchmaker God," who winds the universe up and lets it go. Their god was a God who cares about contingent affairs, loves particular nations, is interested in particular peoples and particular circumstances. Their god was the God of Judaism, the God of Providence. Not a swallow falls in the field but this God knows of it. His action is in the details.

A Fifth Story. The Third Article of the Constitution of Massachusetts:

> As the happiness of a people and the good order and preservation of civil government essentially depend upon piety, religion, and morality, and as these cannot be generally diffused through a community but by the institution of the public worship

of God and of public instructions in piety, religion, and morality: Therefore, To promote their happiness and to secure the good order and preservation of their government, the people of this commonwealth have a right to invest their legislature with power to authorize and require, and the legislature shall, from time to time, authorize and require, the several towns, parishes, precincts, and other bodies-politic or religious societies to make suitable provision, at their own expense, for the institution of the public worship of God and for the support and maintenance of public Protestant teachers of piety, religion, and morality in all cases where such provision shall not be made voluntarily.

When this article was attacked as an infringement on religious liberty, John Adams replied, in effect, "Not at all, you don't have to believe it. But if you want the good order that comes from instruction in religion, particularly the Jewish and Christian religion, then you have to pay for it." That's not the way we think today, I hastily add, but this is the sort of logic our Founders used. Let us walk through the three crucial steps of this logic, one by one.

Right at the beginning of *The Federalist*, in the second paragraph, the author says this generation of Americans is called upon to decide for all time whether governments can be formed "through reflection and choice" or must "forever be formed through accident and force." That's what the Americans were called upon to decide: whether a government may be formed through *reflection* and *choice*.

They then faced the question, How do you institutionalize such a decision? By calling a Constitutional Convention and then having the agreed-upon text ratified in a manner that permits the whole people to participate in the decision. Can there be enough votes for something like that? Can people put aside their regional prejudices? Can they put aside their personal ambitions? Can they think about what's good for the long run? For posterity? That's what *The Federalist* tries to elicit—a long-range view, not what people feel at the moment.

Remember the ambitions of that moment. Many New Yorkers wanted New York to be a separate nation. (The early maps of New York go all the way out to the Pacific Ocean—it's not called "the Empire State" for nothing.) If New York becomes a separate state, it will have its own secretary of state, its own commander in chief, it own secretary of the treasury; distinguished families in New York became ambassadors to the Court of St. James and to Paris and so forth. Such a dream might seem very attractive to some leading families, but would it be good for the country? If New York were to vote to become an independent nation, there could be no union between New England and the South. *Reflection* and *choice* were, then, the hinges of liberty. What Americans *meant* by liberty are those acts that are made from reflection and choice. The acts that we commit ourselves to when we have reflected on the alternatives and when we understand the consequences. That's freedom.

What you do by impulse, by contrast, is not freedom, that's slavery to your impulses. Such slavery is what the animals live under. They're hungry, they need to eat. That's not freedom; it's animal instinct.

Freedom is not doing what you want to do; freedom is doing what, after reflection, you know you *ought* to do. That's what freedom is, and that's why early American thought has been summed up thus: "Confirm thy soul in self-control, Thy liberty in law." Freedom springs from self-government, after reflection and calm deliberate choice.

The second step in the argument is this: To have reflection and choice, you need people with enough virtue to have command of their passions. You need people, that is, with the habits that allow them to reflect, to take time to be dispassionate, to see consequences clearly, and then to make a choice based upon commitment. None of us act that way all the time. But we do aspire to have at least sufficient virtue to live responsibly. For how can a people unable to govern their passions in their private lives, possibly be able to practice self-government in their public lives? It doesn't compute. In short, freedom in a republic is not feasible without virtue.

Next, the third step. George Washington said in his Farewell Address that most people are not going to have virtue or good habits in the long run without religion. And what he meant by that can be recited very simply. As Jews and Christians understand it, religion is not just a cold law; it is a relationship with a person. A person who knows even your secret thoughts. So religion adds a personal motive to the idea of virtue. In addition to that, this Judge sees you even when you're alone, even when you're in secret, even when the doors are closed. This is a Judge who knows whether or not you paint the bottom of the chair. Republics depend on virtue that holds up under such tests. The founding generation used the example of the well-known doctor in Massachusetts who, having been involved in an adultery, turned out also to be a British spy. This was a lesson they often referred to. A man who thinks he can get away with things in secret is not reliable for a republic. A republic cannot be made up of people who think they can do in secret what they wouldn't do in public.

This is why the Founders thought that whatever may be said of persons of "peculiar character," as Washington said (some scholars think he's referring to Jefferson), we must not believe that virtue can be maintained in the long run without religion. Our sons are going to forget about the Revolution, the Founders expected; they're going to forget the suffering we went through. They're going to forget the frozen feet at Valley Forge and the gangrene and the hunger, the lack of pay and the despair. They're going to forget all that, and their grandchildren are going to be tired of hearing it. There's a moral entropy in human affairs, such that even if one generation succeeds in reaching a very high moral level, it's almost impossible for the next generation and the one after that to maintain it. A republic, therefore, has to fight moral entropy. That's why there will have to be a series of moral awakenings. The Founders didn't see how that would happen without religious inspiration, beyond a merely utilitarian impulse.

So there are three principles in this fundamental logic: *No republic without liberty; no liberty without virtue; no virtue without religion.* Now doesn't that sound old-fashioned? In these days, doesn't it sound hardly tenable? Yet our Founders were right. Is not our present circumstance dangerous to the Republic?

The Sixth story. I first heard this story alluded to in Ronald Reagan's Inaugural Address. Dr. Joseph Warren, the family doctor of Abigail and John Adams in Boston, was among the first to join the Sons of Liberty and to stand with the men at Lexington. In fact, he was an officer, and he took a bullet through his hair right above his ear, where it left a crease, but he stood his ground. Two months later, Dr. Warren was commissioned as a major general of the Continental Army. It was a great title, but there wasn't much of an army for the defense of Boston, toward which the British fleet was bringing reinforcements. Dr. Warren learned just four days after he was commissioned that that night the Americans had sent 1,500 men up Bunker Hill. It was one of those still nights when hardly a sound traveled out over the water, where the British fleet was anchored. In the stillness, the troops dug, muffling their shovels, and constructed wooden fortifications, being careful not to strike anything with an axe.

In the morning, the British on board ship awakened to find that Bunker Hill was fortified, and began a five-hour bombardment. Warren heard the bombardment as he was on horseback riding toward Boston, and arrived at Bunker Hill by a back route and managed to climb up into the ranks. He didn't try to take command: he just went into the ranks, in the front rows.

After the bombardment, some of the British soldiers came on land and put Charlestown to the torch, and tongues of flame from 500 homes, businesses, and churches leapt into the sky. Everything in Charlestown burned. Breathless, Abigail Adams watched from a hilltop to the south. She heard the cannons from the warships bombarding Bunker Hill for five long hours as Joseph Warren rode to his position. The American irregulars proved their discipline that day and the accuracy of huntsmen firing in concentrated bursts. They had only four or five rounds apiece. Twice they broke the forward march of thirty-five hundred British troops with fire so withering they blew away as many as 70 to 90 percent of the foremost companies of Redcoats, who lost that day more than a thousand dead.

Then the ammunition of the Americans ran out. While the bulk of the Continental Army retreated, the last units stayed in their trenches to hold off the British hand-to-hand. That is where Major General Joseph Warren was last seen fighting until a close-range bullet felled him. The British officers had him decapitated and bore his head aloft to General Gage.

Freedom is always the most precarious regime. Even a single generation can throw it all away. Every generation must reflect and must choose. Joseph Warren had earlier told the men of Massachusetts at Lexington:

> Our country is in danger now, but not to be despaired of. On you depend the fortunes of America. You are to decide the important questions upon which rest the happiness and the liberty of millions not yet born. Act worthy of yourselves.

THE FOUNDING FATHERS, NATIONAL CHARACTER, AND AMERICAN FOREIGN POLICY

KIM R. HOLMES

As an historian, I always welcome a chance to come to Philadelphia to restore my interest in the early years of the American Republic. And I am most happy to speak to you about the Founding Fathers.

Thinking of the Founding Fathers, I am reminded of a story about Benjamin Franklin and the Constitutional Convention. I am sure some of you have heard it before. After the convention was finished with its work, Franklin was seen leaving the State House by a Mrs. Powel. Seeing Franklin on the street in front of the Hall, she asked, "Well, Doctor, what have we got? A republic or a monarchy?" Franklin replied: "A republic if you can keep it."

How to keep this republic—and how to make it grow and prosper—has been the key question on the minds of many great American leaders.

It was indeed on the mind of George Washington, who said at the end of the Revolution:

> We now stand an Independent People, and have yet to learn political Tactics. We are placed among the Nations on the Earth, and have a character to establish; but how we shall acquit ourselves time must discover.

You can see in this passage something key to understanding not only Washington but all of the Founding Fathers. Washington believed that whether America would survive as a nation—or, to put it another way, whether Franklin's republic would survive—depended on whether our national character thrived and properly informed our policies.

Washington and the Founders believed that the American national character was the key to the Revolution. They believed it unleashed the revolution, sustained the people through the ordeal of the war, and eventually brought them victory.

As they saw it, Americans were a free people bound by a common belief in liberty and a sacred respect for public justice. Washington once said that liberty is the essence of our national character. But what he was pondering in that quote I just gave you is whether we would have the wisdom and prudence to preserve our liberties. And well he should wonder.

I don't think we think often enough these days about the American national character. The Founding Fathers thought about it all the time. They understood that it not only defined who we were as a people, but also showed us in a very practical way what our course should be in the world.

Character encompasses both principle and action. It defines what we stand for and what we are willing to risk for our beliefs. It defines our moral constitution, if you will. In a nation and a leader, character is inseparable from leadership. In many cases, it actually defines it.

Character was, of course, what George Washington was all about. You may recall the story of Washington at the Battle of Monmouth Courthouse in 1778. The Americans were losing the war badly. The British had taken New York and Philadelphia. Washington caught up with the British army at Monmouth, New Jersey, on a very hot summer's day.

One of Washington's lieutenants, Charles Lee, was supposed to make an assault on the British lines, but fearing he was outnumbered withdrew his forces. Washington appeared on the field and upbraided Lee, apparently displaying a terrible streak of temper. After dealing with Lee, Washington took charge of the troops and fought the British to a draw. The British withdrew to New York, turning what was about to be a defeat into a victory—a victory badly needed after a series of stunning defeats.

Lafayette, who was present at the battle, later said: "[Washington] seemed to arrest fortune with one glance." Alexander Hamilton, on his staff at the time, agreed, saying that "[Washington's mere] presence stopped the retreat."

Now, there is more to this story than bravery or even bravado. What is striking is how the reversal of the battle had little or nothing to do with military skill or tactics. Rather, it was almost entirely the result of Washington's character.

I would submit to you that character is no less important to the destiny of leaders than it is to the destiny of nations. Certainly Washington and the other Founding Fathers thought so. They believed that our national character is the essence of our national interest. How well we reflect that character in our policy will determine our destiny as a nation.

What I would like to do today is reflect on how Washington and the other Founders understood the American national character, and ask how that can help us understand better what our place should be in today's world.

There are three great questions that face us today in the making of American foreign policy. They underlie all the great debates, ranging from what to do in Kosovo to how best to relate to the United Nations. They are:

1. What is the purpose of America in the world today?

2. What is her proper role and under what circumstances should she intervene with force?

3. How do we prevent our involvement in world affairs from infringing on our liberties and national sovereignty?

Clinton and Gore would tell you that the purpose of America today is to stop—by force, if necessary—mass killings, avenge human rights abuses, eliminate ethnic and racial hatreds, promote democracy, and serve other so-called humanitarian causes. They believe it is part of our "character" to want to do these things. You can sometimes even hear them invoke the names of the Founding Fathers, particularly Jefferson, in supporting their policies of intervention in Somalia, Haiti, Bosnia, and Kosovo.

But what do the Founding Fathers really say? Let's listen to Washington. He said his aim was that the United States "may be independent of all, and under the influence of none. In a word, I want an American character that the powers of Europe may be convinced we act for ourselves and not for others; this in my judgement, is the only way to be respected abroad and happy at home."

What Washington is saying is that in foreign affairs, we must, above all, protect or own liberties. But Washington and the Founding Fathers also understood that our cause of liberty was not just our own, but the world's. It was, in short, a universal cause for all mankind—a cause they believed received divine blessing. And it was precisely this "universality" and this divine mission that made it just and right—gave it moral purpose, if you will.

As Jefferson once said: "It is impossible not to be sensible that we are acting for all mankind; that circumstances denied to others, but indulged to us, have imposed on us the duty of proving what is the degree of freedom and self-government in which a society may venture to leave its individual members."

In other words, the world is looking to us first to see if the cause of liberty survives. If it works here, it may work anywhere. It is true that America is the beacon and hope for the entire world, but in order for it to shine abroad, it must first be burning bright at home.

This is what Jefferson and the others meant by the "Empire of Liberty": Plant the seed of liberty in the fertile soil of the American continent, nurture it, and let it grow to bear fruit for all the world to enjoy.

Are we not obligated, then, to spread liberty to other peoples and nations?

Yes, but only in a certain fashion. None of the Founding Fathers—not even Thomas Jefferson—ever conceived the cause of American liberty as an imperial crusade, whereby we would force liberty on the rest of the world. At the time of the Founding, of course, we had not the means to do so. But even if we had the power, the Founders would have been reluctant to use it. They feared that too much zeal for spreading liberty abroad could undermine the moral authority of the American cause. The excesses of the French Revolution taught them that power could corrupt the cause of liberty.

But if the Founding Fathers were not "imperialists," neither were they "isolationists,"—at least, not as the term is normally understood today.

Washington, Jefferson, Adams, and Franklin were deft diplomats who engaged in world affairs precisely to safeguard the liberties of the young republic. But since America was very weak at the time of the Founding, they had to play defense. That is why they were concerned about insulating America from too much foreign influence. Their main goal was to prevent the infant country from being drowned in its tub by the great forces raging in Europe at the time of the French Revolution.

But today we live in a different world. We are the most powerful nation on earth. Because our security and interests are global, our cause of liberty is global. Not in the imperial sense, as in forcing it on people, but in the sense that we have to establish an international system in which our own liberty—and thereby the liberties of others—can best flourish.

The true meaning of Washington's warning about foreign entanglements is not to avoid engagement in international affairs, but to prevent that engagement from endangering our liberties. It really is that simple. Washington wanted to prevent foreign meddling from eroding the constitutional order that protected our liberties. He wanted to protect, in a word, our sovereignty.

While Washington and the Founders would not embrace isolationism today, neither would they advocate the utopian internationalism espoused by Bill Clinton and Al Gore. First they would see it as grossly imprudent—as something that cannot be practically accomplished.

But more important, they would see it as a perversion of the cause of liberty. They would be appalled, for example, by our involvement in Balkan politics. In our intervention in Kosovo they would see, as John Quincy Adams once said, "the wars of interest and intrigue, of individual avarice, and envy, an ambition," falsely assuming the "colors and usurped . . . standards of freedom." It is impossible these days to know whose side we are on in Kosovo, but that is precisely the problem: our cause in Kosovo is not really liberty, but social work.

The prudent course for America today is to maintain her strength and to be a world leader. This is the only way to preserve our freedom. Our goal should be to create and sustain an international stability and security in which our own freedom—and with that the freedoms of many others—can flourish.

This does not mean engaging in so-called humanitarian interventions where little if anything humane is accomplished, where much is risked and which demean our ideals with the stench of hypocrisy.

But it does mean maintaining our military alliances with certain key democratic countries to preserve international stability and security.

It does not mean permitting international organizations like the United Nations or the International Criminal Court to encroach on our sovereignty, and thus on our very human rights, as defined by the Constitution.

But it does mean engaging freely in international commerce, as our Founding Fathers advised, to enrich the nation and to create prosperity for all.

And, finally, it does not mean weakening our military and keeping us vulnerable to attack, all because we may falsely believe that others are right to fear us and have reason to believe that our strength will be used against them unjustly, which is what many liberals think.

No, instead it means keeping America militarily strong and doing what is demanded in the Preamble of the Constitution, whereby to provide for the common defense, the first order of business must surely be to do everything in our power to protect the American people from attack.

In this vision of the world, there is no artificial distinction between American national interest and American morality—between idealism and realism. These are false distinctions created by academics who fail to understand the true nature of the American character. It is a vision in which national interest and moral character are one.

- It is moral to keep America strong.
- It is moral to protect our freedom and strength from the debilitating effects of what Adams called "foreign intrigue, avarice and ambition."
- It is moral to protect our liberty—our human rights, if you will—from the interference of foreign bodies, who although they claim they mean well, represent principles not only foreign to our traditions, but harmful to our liberties and to the liberties of others.
- It is moral to do these things because our cause is just and rightly and ultimately the cause of all peoples.

As Jefferson once said: "While we are securing the rights of ourselves and our posterity, we point out the way to struggling nations who wish, like us, to emerge from their tyrannies also."

We should lead *first* by example and *then* by force only when our liberties and security are at stake. That is the great—and still relevant message—of the Founding Fathers.

What does this mean today? What lessons from the Founding Fathers can we apply to problems in today's foreign policy?

I think we can learn a lot. Indeed I have tried to extrapolate some basic principles from which we can justly take some guidance. I think these principles can, and should, inform and guide us as we create a foreign policy agenda appropriate for today's problems.

We have learned that most of the Founders believed in strength. Indeed, that is what is meant by Washington's famous dictum, "there is nothing which will so soon produce a speedy and honorable Peace as a State of preparation for War."

From this it should be crystal clear that we must do all we can to be militarily strong. We are today far weaker than we should be. We need to restore our military strength, to secure the peace and stability in which our liberties can thrive. We should be deploying a defense against nuclear missiles as soon as technically possible. Nothing is more important or more urgent. The threat of missiles to America is real and growing every day. But that would solve only part of the problem of military weakness. We have to cut back on some of Clinton's peacekeeping operations. Our forces are stretched too thin. We are piling military commitments on top of one another, and all the while Clinton cuts the defense budget.

At the same time Clinton has picked fights with tin-pan dictators like Slobodan Milosovic in Serbia, he has appeased the Chinese. He has led them to believe that we would abandon the Taiwanese, and that to trade with them means looking the other way when they abuse human rights, steal our military secrets, or even try to buy our political campaigns. We should deal with China as we deal with any bully in need of reform: Keep the lines of communication open—through trade and political and private contacts—but be firm in the face of intimidation.

We need to start treating Russia differently. Clinton has made the mistake of personalizing politics with Russia. We need to endorse principles, not politicians. We should be standing up for freedom and democracy in Russia, and not tie our hands and our fortunes to the political survival of any one politician.

This agenda stands in stark contrast with that of Bill Clinton and Al Gore. It does so because theirs is based on a different worldview—one that would be foreign to the Founding Fathers. There are real differences of vision between the Clinton administration and us in foreign policy. These different visions produce different policies.

We see an America inspired and guided by Divine Providence and dedicated to the cause of liberty, not only for ourselves, but for others—a liberty founded on virtue and sealed and perpetuated through wisdom and prudence that, altogether, embody our national character.

They see an America moved sometimes by reason, sometimes by unreason, but never by Divine Providence, and dedicated not to liberty, but to the egalitarian principles of the French Revolution, not the American Revolution. They see an America in which self-gratification, not virtue, is the central idea—and an America in which prudence and wisdom are seen not as virtues mediating liberty and creating general happiness, but as vices because they suppress the self-gratification they hold more dear than liberty.

Clinton and Gore believe that a treaty—the ABM Treaty that bans missile defense—with a country that no longer exists is more important than defending Americans from missile attack.

We believe that nothing the government does is more important than protecting our families from the worst holocaust you can ever imagine.

Clinton and Gore believe that it is right to risk thousands of American lives and billions in treasure on causes that are embraced precisely because they have so little value to the defense of American liberty and security.

We believe it is wrong to risk even one American life for such a cause.

And, finally, Clinton apologizes on behalf of Americans to Africans, Guatemalans and Iranians for what he calls the abuses of American power.

We believe that Clinton should be apologizing *to* the American people for his own abuses of power.

These differences define us. And they measure the distance which Clinton and other liberals have traveled not just from the tenets of the conservative movement, but from the traditions of foreign policy first developed by our Founding Fathers.

I don't have any illusions that Clinton and Gore will adopt this agenda of ours. Or that they will accept our view of the Founding Fathers. There is an old proverb that says "Never try to teach a pig to sing. It wastes your time and annoys the pig!"

I would not mind annoying Clinton, but I don't want to waste any time on his singing lessons. Clinton could learn a thing or two from Thomas Paine, who once said "character is much easier kept than recovered." With the President jaunting around the world in search of a new legacy to replace the real, old one, we can rest assured that he is learning just how hard it is to recover from flaws in character.

But the question for us this morning is not whether America can recover from Clinton's personal flaws, but from the "character flaws," if you will, of his foreign policies—flaws, that is, in understanding the true nature of the American national character.

Now, that is truly an open question. I believe we can recover, but it will require a restoration of our understanding of the basic traditions of American foreign policy.

That is where we come in. We at The Heritage Foundation are dedicated to creating a foreign policy based on the traditions that made this country great. We do this in our publications, our work on Capitol Hill, our work with political candidates, with the media and with grass-roots groups all across the country.

The Heritage Foundation provides not only an alternative worldview to Clinton and Gore. We do all we can to make sure that this worldview is put into practice—in Congress, in state and local governments, and, when we have a friendly President, even in the executive branch of the federal government.

We want an America that is strong, free, and independent; that is the vision of our Founding Fathers. It is still our vision at Heritage.

The Heritage Foundation is dedicated to building an America where freedom, opportunity, prosperity, and civil society flourish.

This vision embodies the national character that Washington challenged us to establish over 200 years ago.

Only time will tell whether we will "acquit ourselves" in preserving it.

THE QUIET REPEAL
OF THE AMERICAN REVOLUTION

<hr>

WALTER E. WILLIAMS

Personal liberty, rule of law, and private property protection are values and ideals that have proven elusive for most of mankind's history. Indeed, there are not many ideas older and more common to human history than the notion that the masses should be subject to arbitrary control, abuse, and property confiscation by the powerful elite in pursuit of lofty social goals. In their quest for control, they have used all manner of deceitful rhetoric, emotional manipulation, threats, and brute force.

The framers of our Constitution sought to make a permanent break with that part of mankind's history by erecting barriers between the ruled and the rulers. The U.S. Constitution laid the groundwork for liberty and the rule of law; that is, "government of laws, not of men."

The rule of law implies that rules are known in advance, applied generally, and constrain rulers and the ruled alike. Liberty implies exemptions from the power of rulers and a corresponding limitation on the scope of all laws. For example, the First Amendment to our Constitution says, "Congress shall make no law respecting an establishment of religion, or prohibiting the free exercise thereof; or abridging the freedom of speech, or of the press; or the right of the people peaceably to assemble and to petition the Government for a redress of grievances."

Note that the First Amendment does not say Congress shall grant us rights to freedom of religion, speech, and peaceable assembly. Instead, it says Congress shall make no law respecting or abridging.

The framers of the Constitution believed that there were certain inalienable rights, God-given rights or natural rights that preceded government. Government's job was to guarantee those rights.

The framers had little trust for government and sought to provide us with protections from it. As an aside, I prefer that the framers would have stopped with the fifth word of the Bill of Rights: Congress shall make no law.

Reading through our Constitution, we see that the dominant theme throughout is a healthy distrust of government. Just look at the phraseology: "shall not be infringed," "shall not be violated" "nor shall be compelled," and shall not be: "taken," "disparaged," and "shall not be required. I would venture to say, that when we die and arrive at our next destination, if we see anything resembling our Constitution and the Bill of Rights we know that we are in Hell. Such distrustful language would be an affront to God.

The essence of the American Revolution was not to overthrow one set of rulers and put another in power, nor was it to replace one public policy agenda with another. The essence of the American Revolution was a wholesale rejection of the notion of the divine right of kings, where the sovereigns were seen as having been given their right to rule by God, and were thus not accountable to their subjects.

The American Revolution and the Constitution that it gave birth to sought to lay down a set of restraints on whoever held the power to rule. Tragically, today's Americans are running away from the ideals of the American Revolution at a breakneck speed.

My good friend and colleague Dr. Thomas Sowell, in his most recent book, *The Quest for Cosmic Justice*, cites a quotation from Alexis de Tocqueville that goes a long way towards explaining why our Constitution is under increasing, unrelenting attack. Alexis de Tocqueville said:

> It may be easily seen that almost all the able and ambitious members of a democratic community will labor unceasingly to extend the powers of government, because they all hope at some time or other to wield those powers themselves.

The rule of law is seen as an obstacle by the nation's elite. The rule of law is not the same as rules having an equal impact on all. Sowell says that those in pursuit of cosmic justice view the latter as an injustice. Thus, courts have ruled that hiring procedures, racially neutral on their face, that have a "disparate impact" are racially discriminatory.

What a court may see as discriminatory is not spelled out in advance. A good example is what constitutes not taking "reasonable" measures to accommodate the employment of mentally or physically handicapped individuals. What is the correct percentage of minority and women employees is not spelled out in advance. A defendant finds out, for example, what the "reasonable" measures are to accommodate the handicapped, after he has been charged with discrimination and perhaps fined millions of dollars. This, Sowell says, represents ex post facto law, expressly forbidden by the Constitution.

Sowell says among the constitutional barriers limiting the expansion of federal government powers is the Tenth Amendment, which says, "The powers not delegated to the United States by the Constitution, nor prohibited by it to the States, are reserved to the States respectively, or to the people." This barrier to the expansion and consolidation of central government power is one of the fundamental protections of freedom and epitomizes the spirit of the American Revolution.

The framers said that the federal government can only do what it has been authorized to do by the Constitution and nothing else. Indeed, this was a concern among the delegates to the Constitutional Convention in 1787. They openly expressed fears that the Constitution as drafted would lead to consolidation of power and they urged that the Constitution not be ratified unless it ultimately contained protections such as the Tenth Amendment.

Sowell says that the New Deal and an expansive interpretation of the Constitution's "commerce clause" by the U.S. Supreme Court has turned the Tenth Amendment into a dead letter. Here, I think my colleague is only partially correct. The groundwork that made the Tenth Amendment a dead letter came much earlier—in 1865, at the end of the "War between the States," popularly known as the Civil War.

The War between the States settled, by force, that states did not have the right to secede, nor could they nullify unconstitutional acts by the federal government. Once these states' response to a heavy-handed government were ruled out, it became possible for the federal government to escape its status as the agent and creation of the states.

The original purpose of the Constitution has been reversed: States have become creatures of the federal government, and the federal government has assumed supremacy. Look at the attack on our Second Amendment guarantees. Whenever there's a tragedy involving gun use, Bill Clinton, Al Gore, America's assorted leftists, and the news media seize it as another opportunity to exploit the emotions of uninformed American people for political gain.

Unfortunately, most Americans don't have the foggiest notion of why the framers of the Constitution, through the Second Amendment, guaranteed our right to keep and bear arms. Leftists would like us to believe the Second Amendment was written to protect our right to go deer and duck hunting. But don't take my word for it; let's look at what was actually said during the debates on ratifying the Constitution. Thomas Jefferson said, "No man shall ever be debarred the use of arms. The strongest reason for the people to retain the right to keep and bear arms is, as a last resort, to protect themselves against tyranny in government."

Tench Coxe, assistant secretary of the Treasury (1789), said, "The unlimited power of the sword is not in the hands of either the federal or state governments, but, where I trust in God it will ever remain, in the hands of the people."

Noah Webster said, "The supreme power in America cannot enforce unjust laws by the sword, because the whole body of the people are armed, and constitute a force superior to any band of regular troops."

In Federalist Paper No. 46, James Madison said "the Constitution preserves the advantage of being armed which Americans possess over the people of almost every other nation, the existence of subordinate governments, to which the people are attached, forms a barrier against the enterprises of ambition...."

Many sentiments like these were expressed during the ratification debates. But, here's my question: Which one of them sounds like the framers had deer and duck hunting in mind when they gave us the Second Amendment? No, the framers gave us the Second Amendment so we could have, at least, a last ditch fighting chance against our government's encroachment on our liberties.

Who are the people who want to disarm law-abiding Americans? It's not rocket science to figure that one out. The strongest advocates of gun control are the very people who seek more and more control over our lives. They are the very Americans who want to take away our rights to property, freedom of speech and religion, and other constitutional guarantees. They figure if we're first disarmed they can do it with impunity.

What needs to be done to recapture our liberties or preserve what is left? First, we must learn what the Constitution permits and does not permit. After all, the Constitution represents our rules of the game, and if we do not know the rules, we can be cheated or misled. Now there are some who say that our Constitution is a living document. That, my friends, is equivalent to saying that we have no Constitution at all and the rules are made up as we go along.

How many of you would play poker with me, where the rules are made up as we play, or, in other words, are "living." Maybe a circumstance will arise where my two-pair, in contrast to the "Hoyle's Rules," beat your full house.

Knowing what the Constitution permits and does not permit will allow us to make the appropriate response to federal edicts. I, for one, believe that no one has a moral obligation to obey unconstitutional or immoral edicts and laws. But if a person opts to go that route, he must be prepared to face the consequences.

There is another possible solution that I have been thinking about lately. It might be a harebrained idea. But I think liberty-minded people ought to populate several contiguous states in large numbers and then secede from the Union. I think secession has a greater potential for peace than the alternative. That alternative being one group of Americans attempting to forcibly impose their will on another group, and that group attempting to resist as much as possible. Why not simply part company? The first secession was a success (that from England) and the second a failure (the War between the States). I say why not break the tie?

THE FATE OF CONSTITUTIONAL GOVERNMENT

CHARLES R. KESLER

My theme is constitutional government in America, then and now. I'd like to give you some idea of the condition of constitutional government in the United States after a century of critique and demolition.

The place to begin is with some large and familiar truths about the genesis and character of the American constitutional system. It's important to realize that our Constitution, the Constitution of 1787, written only a few blocks from here, was not the first American constitution. State constitutions had blossomed during the Revolution, and the Articles of Confederation, written in 1776–77, had finally been ratified by the states in 1781. The Articles was our first national constitution, and was already in an advanced state of decay and collapse by the time the delegates, headed by George Washington, assembled in Philadelphia in May 1787 to try to write a new and improved Constitution for the United States.

We ought to reflect on the fact that our first attempt at a national constitution was unsuccessful. It helps us to appreciate the storied success of our second and still reigning constitutional document. But we should never forget that the first one suffered from many weaknesses—"imbecilities," as the people of the time called them—and that in the state governments, injustice and instability were rampant.

The delegates who met during the summer of 1787 were looking to devise a stronger, more energetic national government than the one that then existed. Though energetic, the proposed new government would be limited in its objects, so that its strength and activity would be directed only towards a few great national concerns, things like national defense, interstate commerce, diplomacy—large objects that had to be addressed at the national level, not local questions of administration that were left for the state governments to deal with.

The Constitution approved by the Philadelphia convention on September 17, 1787 was thus our second constitution, but it did not mark the beginning of a new regime. And so unlike the French, we haven't had to number our republics. We still like to think we live in the same Republic that was born in 1776 and reformed in 1787–88. But as I'll try to show in just a minute, that is a boast that has now become questionable.

The republic that was bequeathed to us in 1787 was a representative republic, the first representative republic, really, in human history. According to the Constitution, "We the People" are the source of all political authority in American politics, but the people are not a branch of the federal government. In every preceding republic, the "people" *was* the government or a part of it. If you visit Rome, for example, you will see placards on the side of ancient buildings that say "SPQR" (*senatus populusque Romanus*)—the Senate and the

People of Rome. These were essentially the two branches of the Roman government. The senate was one part; the people, the other. The people were in turn organized into two or three different kinds of assemblies, but when an assembly convened, every citizen had the right and duty to attend.

In America, the people does not constitute a branch or a part of our government; they constitute the authority for all its branches. In other words, we hire folks, as Ross Perot used to say, to run the government for us. In this way, the American people's opinion is made sovereign over the whole government, so that our form of government is wholly popular.

The people's sovereignty is expressed in regular elections held in accordance with the Constitution's provisions, but the people don't have to intervene directly to check and balance the parts of government because our Constitution enables the parts to check and balance each other.

The Constitution's framers and ratifiers recognized two aspects of this balance. States have a kind of residual sovereignty, and their power helps to balance that confided to the central government. The other—probably more important— balance was within the new constitution itself: the famous separation of powers, which the Americans brought to a kind of perfection in 1787 and 1788.

Separation of powers has three purposes. The first purpose, obviously, is to prevent tyranny—to prevent any one branch of government from encroaching on the other branches, in order to keep government as a whole in its proper place. This is, you might say, the negative function of the separation of powers: to prevent "over-government," or tyranny. The second purpose is to allow each branch of the government to perform its characteristic function well, to do its peculiar job excellently, which calls for a strong presidency that would possess energy in the administration of the government; a bicameral legislature arranged in such a way as to enable it both to be representative and to deliberate about laws intelligently; and an independent judiciary that would decide the meaning of the law in particular cases.

The third function of the separation of powers, and in a way the most important function, is to enable the people to develop a reverence for the Constitution. James Madison explained in *The Federalist* that a proper separation of powers encourages the branches of government to check one another so that the people won't have to be continually intervening in order to fix the government. Precisely because we don't have to continually interpret and repair the Constitution, we may begin to revere it. Although we establish it by our own consent, it's such a good Constitution that we rarely have to do anything with it except live under it and thus try to live up to it.

So here is perhaps the greatest accomplishment of the American founding. The American people made a new Constitution and form of government for themselves, but unlike most other republics in human history, they have been able to live under and live up to that Constitution ever since, because they haven't regarded it simply as statute law that could be changed easily and often whenever the whim hit them.

To see the great contrast between this kind of Constitution and the other kind, you might think of the California Constitution, a "living Constitution" if there ever was one. I had lived in California for probably 13 or 14 years before I ever saw a copy of the California Constitution, which gives you some idea of how significant it is. The California Constitution is, literally, a book, and every two years we amend it through initiatives and referenda of various kinds. The result is that no one looks up to the California Constitution. The California Constitution is, in effect, a way to get public policy objectives enacted when one can't get them through the legislature. And so it tends to become merely a means to our political ends—an instrument of our political passions, not a form of higher law that might discipline our desires.

When we look more broadly at American government today, we really have to wonder whether we are living in the Republic founded by George Washington and James Madison, or whether we're in fact living in a new Republic. This Second Republic (the French may have something to teach us after all!) began about a hundred years ago, and its most visible and clear-sighted representative is probably Woodrow Wilson.

President Wilson was an academic before he became a president, and he did wonderful damage in both capacities. Wilson was the first president to have an academic theory (not just an interpretation) of the Constitution, which came right out of Charles Darwin and German political science. Wilson was also the first president to criticize the Constitution as a whole.

His basic argument was that the Constitution was obsolete or, at best, increasingly obsolete. It was an 18th-century document incapable of solving 20th-century problems, and so Wilson tried to build a bridge from the 18th to the 20th century, even as a more recent president wanted to extend that bridge into the 21st century.

Wilson charged that the Constitution was Newtonian, designed as if human nature were governed by permanent forces of selfishness (analogous to the law of gravity) that could be played off against one another. The government would be then like a solar system in which every branch was held rigidly in place, resulting in political deadlock or gridlock. Wilson insisted, by contrast, that government should be interpreted in light of Darwin, not Newton. Government was not a machine, but a living thing, an organism, and so America deserved a "living Constitution" if its politics were to keep pace with the times.

Wilson is really the inventor of the living constitution theory, which is not, as we tend to think of it today, a theory mainly about the judiciary and how judges ought to interpret the Constitution. For Wilson it was a comprehensive theory about the whole Constitution, in which all the branches of government have to be regarded as changeable and adaptable. Instead of a "limited Constitution" that reflects certain truths about human nature, and therefore is meant to be as permanent as possible, government ought to reflect the continual changes in human nature and thus must itself have no definite form but be able to grow and adapt indefinitely.

Human rights change over time, according to Wilson, and so the Constitution must change over time. The natural and God-given rights invoked in the Declaration of Independence were, then, neither natural nor God-given but instead all too human—cultural artifacts of the 18th century.

Freedom, therefore, is not a natural right but a social right. In fact, individuals as such don't exist by nature. Individuals are social and historical creations. When left to themselves, individuals are weak until lifted to freedom by government. Human freedom is not the source of government; personal freedom is the product of government.

Human beings don't, therefore, have an inborn spirit of freedom; we don't have what it takes to govern ourselves by nature. That has to be infused in us because by nature we are weak, almost non-existent. Now this is somewhat hard to understand. So let me bring it home by citing a paragraph from President Clinton's last State of the Union Address. Clinton liked to pick out people in the gallery to celebrate. He picked out Hank Aaron, for example, as well as others not nearly as well known as Hank Aaron, and here is one of them.

Clinton was talking about child support payments and getting fathers to support their children:

> We should recognize that a lot of fathers want to do right by their children, but need help to do it. Carlos Rosus, of St. Paul, Minnesota, wanted to do right by his son, and he got the help to do it. Now he's got a good job and he supports his little boy. My budget will help 40,000 more fathers make the same choices Carlos Rosus did. I thank him for being here tonight. [Applause] Stand up Carlos. Thank you. [More applause]

Mr. Rosus is basically a guy who got a job. The tremendous step forward he has taken is to get a job to support his family, and this is something that is so extraordinary that he has to be recognized in the State of the Union Address. Of course he didn't get a job by himself; he got it through government assistance in a vague way that Clinton never specifies. Modern liberalism presumes that men are too weak even to get a job in order to support their families without being reconstructed or supported by government in some way. That's how weak our love of freedom really is.

Two revolutionary changes swept over American government in the past hundred years. The first concerned federalism. Federalism is in dire straits. Beginning with the New Deal, the Commerce Clause became an all-purpose excuse for the expansion of federal regulatory power. The result was to centralize power in Washington so as to create, for the first time in American history, a centralized form of administration.

Another blow dealt the federalism of the original Constitution was the 17th Amendment, providing for the direct election of senators rather than their indirect election by state legislatures. Federalism's chief institutional safeguard was thereby abolished. There is no organic connection now between the state governments and the national government, and as a result there is much less resistance among the states to the expansion of federal power.

The second epic transformation involved American republicanism. For the American Founders, the goal of government was to secure our natural rights. Nowadays, the purpose of government is not so much to secure our natural rights as to provide us new rights, to bestow on us social and economic and other kinds of entitlements—the list goes on and on, and it's still being added to.

In another way, republicanism has changed because of the pressure on separation of powers. In order to bring us to a higher moral and political consummation (to borrow Herbert Croly's phrase), the limitations of separation of powers had to be overcome and the spirit of checks and balances had to yield to the spirit of unchecked government power. The differences in the nature of the three powers, therefore, had to be denied. When FDR assailed the Supreme Court after the 1936 election, he described the three branches of government as the three horses pulling the people's chariot. He implied that there was no difference in kind between judicial and legislative power, or between judicial and executive power. It was all a matter of sheer horsepower, but the judicial horse was a little froward—it needed to be whipped into line, which is in effect what FDR did.

So today the three branches of government are not there to perform specific functions in pursuit of the common good, all the while restraining each other from tyranny. On the contrary, the branches must cooperate in the unremitting exercise of a general government power that is beneficent and does not, therefore, need to be limited or restrained. And because the powers of government are so interchangeable, they can be easy delegated. The legislature can give power to the executive, and the executive can give power to the courts without compunction.

The separation of powers really does tend to break down in modern American government. You can see this most clearly in the regulatory agencies, which not only have the power to issue regulations but also to enforce them and to judge infractions of them. The agencies have legislative, executive, and judicial power all in the same set of unelected hands. Having all three powers in the same set of hands would be, for the Founders, the very definition of tyranny.

Now, given the collapse of constitutional barriers, what remains to help the American people limit government? Well, the courts will occasionally strike down the most obnoxious insults against the Constitution, but the most effective check left is the consent of the governed. We still have elections and they can still make a big difference.

But even the people's consent has been partially transformed by modern liberalism. The governed now have to be led, have to be managed, by leaders. Increasingly, the president becomes familiar to us not as a constitutional officer whose highest job is to enforce and perpetuate the Constitution, but as a kind of charismatic champion of new rights and new government benefits. In the course of the 20th century, we grew accustomed to looking to the president for visions of the political future, towards which he would graciously lead us. We have a kind of visionary politics we never had before. The first President Bush had a famous problem with the "vision thing," a disability that was in many ways admirable. He didn't believe that the purpose of government was to go off on whatever damn fool crusade someone had thought up that morning or dreamed up the night before. In his eyes, the purpose of the presidency was to run the government, that is to administer the constitutional office in a constitutional way.

Given almost a century's worth of liberal innovations, it's not surprising that American politics looks increasingly post-constitutional. We hardly talk about the Constitution in our politics any more. And our political parties don't justify themselves by trying to defend the Constitution the way they did throughout the 19th and early 20th centuries. In fact, we hardly hear the parties take a position on the interpretation of the Constitution except on the narrow (though important) question of what kind of judges ought to be appointed. But it's clear that judges alone cannot restore constitutionalism to American politics.

In fact, we need three branches of government that are interested in restoring constitutionalism, and to effect that revolution we need political parties willing to take a stand on behalf of the original Constitution and against the new Constitution of the Second Republic.

THE FOUNDERS'
FOREIGN POLICY AND ITS BETRAYAL

HON. MALCOLM WALLOP

The task to discuss the Founders and the beginnings of American foreign policy has been exhilarating. To reread the writings of Thomas Paine, Adams, Hamilton, George Washington, Madison, and Jefferson is to visit the treasure trove of wisdom, decency, morality, virtue, and passion that was the unique character they nurtured at every instance in the America they founded. It was not as though they cheerfully agreed on everything.

Their passions and ambitions were high and they were resolute chaps as Hamilton discovered with Aaron Burr. But I must say that to reread them in the light of today's pathetic excuse for policy is to vacillate between unbounded rage and a sort of forlorn sadness that we have allowed so great a heritage to be squandered almost beyond retrieval.

Every one of the Founders believed that the fortunes of America in the world depended upon the American people's uncommon strength of character, virtue, and deep sense of morality. They believed that the Creator, who endowed us all with inalienable rights, demanded virtue and prudence as the price of freedom.

Let me try to define for you what foreign policy was to them, and should be for us. Foreign policy was the projection of America's interests and her character abroad. It included her national security and honor, her national economy, and the safety of her citizens abroad. Foreign policy involved risking the lives of citizens, and they alone could decide to accept that risk. This implied above all a certain prudence and discretion. It meant caring for the struggles of other countries by wishing them well without taking sides. It contained the realization that without divine blessings and great exertions of their own, foreigners could not achieve the kinds of liberties Americans alone enjoyed. They believed that virtue and righteousness made popular government possible, not the reverse. America's foreign commitments were to be few and solemn.

The foundations of American policy were conceived long before the Revolutionary War. The war was about trade and the systematically denied trading rights of the colonists. The war was about taxes without reason. The war was about the denial of self-government where it had long existed. The war was about the attempt to disarm the colonials. The war was about expropriating property that the crown had never owned, only to bestow it upon those who had never won it. Most importantly, the war was about denying those natural rights endowed not by London but by our Creator. The Americans' assertion of these rights and interests in the context of the war was the birth of American foreign policy. George Washington in earlier days had been inclined to socialize with the British rulers and military officers and resist the concept of Independence until he read the greatest treatise on America, Americans, and American polity ever written: Thomas Paine's *Common Sense*.

Thomas Paine argued that the revolution was not about restoring justice for the colonists or even about money. It was about establishing a new nation conceived as all nations should be, but only America could be. He wrote:

> Taking up arms, merely to enforce the repeal of a pecuniary law, seems as unwarrantable by the divine law, and as repugnant to human feelings, as the taking up arms to enforce obedience thereto. The object on either side doth not justify the means; for the lives of men are too valuable to be cast away on such trifles.

As to the choice of independence over mere rebellion:

> But what must weigh most with all men of serious reflection are the moral advantages arising from Independence. War and desolation have become the trade of the Old World: and America neither can nor could be under the government of Britain without becoming a partner in the dismal commerce of death. 'Tis the natural temper of Britain to fight for a feather if they supposed that feather to be an affront and America without the right of asking why must have abetted in every quarrel and abided by its fate. It certainly ought to be a conscious as well as a political consideration with America not to dip her hands in the bloody work of Europe.

Here in a nutshell is the rationale for the Senate's role in ratifying treaties and for Congress's exclusive power in declaring war. The Founders wanted no unilateral power to craft national commitments because they could not accept subjecting citizens to the mixed jurisdiction of foreign and domestic courts. And the use of American force could only be decided by the citizens themselves because their God-given lives were at stake.

The concept of the consent of the governed was essential. In a sermon, Samuel Cooper noted that "even the Law of Moses, though framed by God Himself, was not imposed upon the people against their will: it was laid before the whole congregation of Israel and they freely adopted it." There began the one constant in American foreign policy until President Wilson shamefully abandoned it: respect for the common man, neutrality, and the rationalization of ends to means.

Washington's passionate goal was to establish a unified and virtuous nation with a national character of probity. The lives of the people were precious, and only to be hazarded by the consent of the people themselves. In his view, the original point of foreign policy was to foster the American people's unity and love for America. To this end he had sought in every way to keep the Revolutionary War from becoming a civil war and foreign quarrels from becoming bones of contention within America. Our neutrality was designed to keep the population from taking sides.

Under Washington there would be no hunt for anti-government Americans. Nor, in an America filling up with Germans, Frenchmen, Jews, Irish, and so forth, would there be any policy but American policy in which all could share. He dismissed the French ambassador for trying to recruit Americans to the French Revolution on the grounds that this was an intolerable intrusion into national unity. And in military matters, he taught that alliances were only useful if they served well-calibrated purposes, and the first of these was not to extend beyond their means the limited forces the young nation possessed.

Ours was not a nation to gain dominion over the world. It would be difficult enough to keep ourselves virtuous. Washington agreed with Paine that "virtue is not hereditary." Hear John Adams reflecting a common theme among the Founders: "Constitutional defects flow generally from the defects of spirit and morality among the people which a revolution in government could not reform." He contrasted America with Europe. We were a nation of inalienable rights as compared with theirs of inalienable allegiance. There was a moral supremacy of the people. Truths that were self-evident conveyed principles and rights bestowed by God. These were inalienable and no government could ravish them. Foreign policy was linked to domestic unity and again unity to strength.

Thomas Paine wrote: "A nation despicable by its weakness forfeits even the privilege of being neutral." Thus the first goal of securing means was securing the support of the people. The new nation after the war sought restoration of trade. It needed economic as well as military strength, and economic strength came as much as anything from private property and free trade. And, Pat Buchanan notwithstanding, the only protected commerce was gun manufacturing. The more guns in the hands of a virtuous people the better.

For military strength they realized that since they no longer fell under the protection of the crown they needed a navy. But to what end? Jefferson wanted it to attack the Barbary pirates because he was tired of paying their ransom for trade. Others argued that even supposing we could whack them hard, we lacked the power to sustain our presence and soon would have to pay up again. The means were beyond us. The ends became the security of our harbors and our trading. We were to become the arbiters of Europe in America through our navy. Paine observed: "Britain's navy gives her check over U.S. Trade in Europe, but ours a check over hers in the Indies."

In *The Federalist Papers,* Hamilton argues tirelessly for national strength through national unity: "Let the thirteen states ... concur in erecting one great American system, superior to the control of all transatlantic forces or influence, and able to dictate the terms of the connection between the old and the new world." And, "there is no justification in being so weak as to invite disaster, but there is an exacting obligation to use only so much power as is necessary to protect liberty."

Wars raged in Europe both territorial and revolutionary. The support of the fledgling nation was sought by all sides. Hamilton and Jefferson argued as to whether or not we ought to support France over Britain. Jefferson said that we had a moral obligation in as much as they had sided with us in our revolution, and besides, "if we withheld support we would give France a just cause of war and so become associated with the other side." But Hamilton's view was that France's support had been less to aid America than to confound Britain. He argued for neutrality, counseling against entanglements that "rashly mingle our destiny in the consequences of the errors and extravagances of another nation."

In his farewell address, George Washington issued a declaration of diplomatic independence, arguing for our separation from the politics of Europe and for policies that avoided all concepts of moral and ideological preference which might prejudice the nation's freedom of choice. Our trading relations should be in their words "open, equal, and multilateral." That is why Americans wished the world well but did not try to impose their government. To state this view clearly John Quincy Adams wrote: "I am not an enthusiast who wishes to overturn empires and monarchies for the sake of introducing republican forms of government, and equally I am no king killer nor king hater."

But he and the founding generations were passionate lovers of America. We sought no territorial conquests, nor would we even accept the voluntary accession of states either through gifts or referendum or trades. Thus we rejected the Yucatan because its people lacked the capacity to live freely under the Constitution, but accepted Texas because they clearly had the capacity. We would, at the same time, resist the empirical expansion of Europe in our hemisphere. We would as soon as possible, recognize the independence of South American countries.

John Quincy Adams was in effect the drafter of the Monroe Doctrine, a unilateral declaration that followed our rejection of a British proposal to make a similar declaration jointly. If we were to become identified with British interests in South America, our relations with the others would be impaired. Besides, our interests and our approach to the world were different. We could easily have annexed Cuba, which was, and will always be, very important to us. But we never wanted to do it for the same reason we did not want to take Mexico. Nor was it in our interest to see Cuba fall to Britain. So although the Monroe Doctrine could not bring good government to our hemisphere—indeed, nothing could have—it safeguarded American interests without compromising our principles. John Quincy Adams believed that self-preservation was an obligation paramount to every other law. Foreign military power in our hemisphere threatened self-preservation. America would never seek to rule and therefore could never colonize. Adams then issued 14 fundamentals of U.S. interests. Among these were the following: 1) Sovereign Independence 2) Freedom of the Seas 3) Freedom of Commerce and Navigation 4) Stay Out of Europe's Wars 5) There Were To Be No Transfers from One Colonial Power to Another. 6) No Further European Colonization of the New World. 7) Anti Imperialism for America 8) Europe To Keep Hands Off America. 9)

Free Rights of Expatriation and Naturalization 10) Suppression of the Slave Trade.

These principles served the young nation well. The exceptions proved the rule. For example, beginning in the 1830s, Americans began to abandon free trade, and to use the tariff not just to raise money but for protectionism. This added to the growing gulf between the North and the South, and contributed to the Civil War. Of all that could be said of how Lincoln's statesmanship during the Civil War followed the precepts laid down by the founding generation, I will touch on just one: that in any struggle, the primordial objective must be to enhance the American people's unity and virtue. When the South Carolina legislature voted to secede, Lincoln's first action was to call a joint session of Congress to hear the reading aloud of the first nine Federalist Papers (those that deal with unity). Lincoln practiced what Washington had taught. The greatest enemy was not the Confederate army, any more than the British army had been for Washington. Rather, the enemy to be defeated was the ill feeling that some Americans had for others. Hence Lincoln fought America's bloodiest war always with an eye on peace. Even the Emancipation Proclamation affected only areas still under rebel control. Moreover, he refused to call what the South had done "secession," and kept up the pretense that the Union could not be broken. Hence Southern senators and congressmen were invited to take up their seats in the Capitol. Had he lived, there probably would not have been the Reconstruction, for he would not have tolerated the division of the people as victor and vanquished. Unity would have been his immediate goal.

From Lincoln's time right through to Teddy Roosevelt, American presidents managed our affairs with respect and admiration for the people, and with singular restraint in the foreign affairs of the nation. Then like the flash of light before a bulb burns out, Teddy Roosevelt epitomized the search for virtue and unbounded admiration for his countrymen. His leadership of an America that had become the world's greatest power showed how wrong are those who today attribute the founding generation's prudent foreign policies to early America's weakness.

Roosevelt's record shows just how possible it is to uphold national honor and pride in virtue without posturing, as he did with regard to the Russian pogroms in 1902. He demonstrated how to foster peace without presuming to dictate its terms as he did with regard to the Russo–Japanese War of 1905. He exhibited rare skills in applying the use of American power in defense of an essential national interest as he advised doing with the looming conflict in Europe in 1914.

Then along came Woodrow Wilson. It is important to note that Roosevelt's America had been no less powerful than the one Wilson committed to war. The differences were principles, prudence, and restraint. The compellingly ugly act of Woodrow Wilson, after the defeat of the League of Nations, was to blame Americans for the problems of the world. It became, in the century just past, the common thread of presidents and Secretaries of State, including the likes of Henry Kissinger, to complain that the American people's defining characteristics hamper statecraft. Their predecessors viewed them as the nation's greatest source of strength.

The power that the United States has brought to bear on the world in the twentieth century is comparable only to that of history's greatest empires. But since World War I, the ends of American policy have been incomparably more ambitious than those of the Romans, Mongols, the Spanish, and the British. Insofar as it aims to end war and to establish a particular way of life throughout the globe, the foreign policy of the United States is comparable only to that of the old Soviet Union. No earthly power would ever suffice to achieve the ends set forth by even the most modest of American presidents since Woodrow Wilson.

It is not surprising that many American policy-makers have made careers by making promises they could not keep and threats they could not carry out. They have pursued their ends on the cheap. They have become uncomfortable with the very concept of America's national interest, and they have become impatient with the American people's reluctance to lend themselves to their projects.

Despite weakness and vulnerability, early Americans gloried in their differences from the rest of the world. Nevertheless in their dealings with foreign nations they pursued the national interest with classic sobriety. In this century however, even as our statesmen have de-emphasized our differences from the rest of the world, or even deprecated the inflexibility of American morals, American foreign policy has been characterized by ideas and practices that violate the timeless norms of statecraft.

Instead of living by Caesar Augustus's dictum: "Shorten your borders and strengthen your legions," or Teddy Roosevelt's classic expression of the Founders' wisdom, "Speak softly and carry a big stick," American foreign policy has invented any number of concepts by which it has slipped the leash that is supposed to bind ends and means. You know them as "collective security," "arms control," "peacekeeping," "nation building," "mutual assured destruction," and "constructive engagement." We have assigned thaumaturgic powers to democracy, to commerce, and to communications.

Virtually alone in this century, Ronald Reagan admired Americans, understood strength, and sought our support. For his legacy, the Cold War ended in a classic application of strength and principle while minimizing risk. The Clinton administration understands only polls, not power; corruption, not virtue. It crafts its policy as favors to foreign or domestic constituencies. It constantly divides us by herding Americans into any number of classifications and sets us to competing one with another for their favors. It commits Americans in harm's way, then insist that America's reputation demands that Congress endorse their recklessness.

America's respect and reputation abroad is at its all time low. Oh, my friends, what a sorry way to start a new century, let alone a millennium. The saving grace, as you know, will always be Americans in their towns and cities, on their farms, in their mines and factories, at work and at prayer. Americans are yet a people more virtuous, more courageous, and more wise than those who lead them.

My prayer is this: Dear God, please continue to bless America.

WOULD THE FOUNDING FATHERS BE HAPPY WITH AMERICA TODAY?

ROBERT H. BORK

The topic assigned me is, Would the Founders be pleased with the condition of American today? The answer is yes and no. Rather than sit down with that succinct summary, I will take a moment to expand on that conclusion.

Given the inestimable benefits of hindsight, it seems obvious that the Founders were bound to be disappointed in some of their fondest hopes, that much of our divergence from the original plan was inevitable. We will have to live with that; there is no point in nostalgia for the Founders' vision when experience shows us that that vision was bound to be thwarted in major respects.

The most disappointed would be Thomas Jefferson. His hopes for a country of yeomen, or small farmers—self-reliant, socially equal, free of the vices that cities, manufacturing, and financial power would bring—was doomed from the start. American drive and ingenuity, coupled with a sense of adventure and a desire for better material lives, were bound to create the economic giant he feared. The future belonged to Alexander Hamilton.

Yet, if Jefferson's hopes were unrealistic, his fears were not entirely so. The Founders understood the need for civic virtue in a democracy. They did not think that formal democratic institutions would be enough, and they were right. James Madison, among others, was very clear on that point. It is impossible to devise a mechanical system so perfect that nobody has to be good. Many nations have constitutions that on paper are as democratic and devoted to liberty as ours but remain in conditions of chaos and corruption. One has only to look at South American nations that, despite such constitutions, are often ruled by oligarchies or military juntas. The Soviet Union used to boast that its constitution guaranteed much greater human freedom and happiness than ours, and we know the horrible reality that hid behind the words.

The sources of civic virtue and the conditions for its maintenance are complex topics, and I realize that what I have to say next is an oversimplification; yet it contains important truths nonetheless. Many of the Founders also thought that the long-run health of civic virtue depended on vibrant religion. The fact that America is the most church-going nation in the world should not mislead us.

Religion today has been invaded by the therapeutic heresy, according to which its function is not to enjoin moral behavior so much as to provide personal comfort. Many churches impose fewer and fewer obligations but keep assuring people that God loves them. I am sure He does, though it must be a considerable strain with respect to some of them. People who should not be are quite content with the condition of their souls.

A recent poll asked people to rate those most likely to be welcomed into heaven. Mother Theresa came in second with

73 percent of the votes. You may have difficulty in guessing who came in first. Themselves, with 87 percent of the votes.

Much of the decline of real belief is due to an overwhelmingly secular intellectual class, by which I mean not only university faculties but also journalists, Hollywood, and the courts—all of which have proved persistently hostile to religion. Justice Potter Stewart put the matter well in a lone dissent:

> [A] compulsory state educational system so structures a child's life that if religious exercises are held to be an impermissible activity in schools, religion is placed at an artificial and state-created disadvantage. . . . [P]ermission of such exercises for those who want them is necessary if the schools are to be truly neutral in the matter of religion. And a refusal to permit religious exercises thus is seen, not as the realization of state neutrality, but rather as the establishment of a religion of secularism . . . ."

That is true and it is devastating. The late Christopher Lasch, a man of the left, asked "what accounts for [our society's] wholesale defection from the standards of personal conduct—civility, industry, self-restraint—that were once thought indispensable to democracy?" He answered that a major reason is the "gradual decay of religion." Our liberal elites, whose "attitude to religion," Lasch said, "ranges from indifference to active hostility" have succeeded in removing religion from public recognition and debate.

That has had consequences. According to James Q. Wilson: "In the mid-nineteenth century England and America reacted to the consequences of industrialization, urbanization, immigration, and affluence by asserting an ethos of self-control, whereas in the late twentieth century they reacted to many of the same forces by asserting an ethos of self-expression."

The difference between the two centuries was the presence in the nineteenth of religion and church-related institutions that inculcated morality and civic virtue.

It may be no accident that the decline of civic virtue in our time occurred almost simultaneously with the cultural revolution that began to sweep America in the 1960s. The trends had been apparent for some time but the Sixties vastly accelerated them and the result was a decline in personal morality, which is certainly connected to civic virtue. Roger Kimball wrote, accurately I think, of the depth and power and devastation wrought by that revolution:

> [T]he radical emancipationist demands of the Sixties [have] triumphed throughout society. They have insinuated themselves, disastrously, into the curricula of our schools and colleges; they have dramatically altered the texture of sexual relations and family life; they have played havoc with the authority of churches and other repositories of moral wisdom; they have undermined the claims of civic virtue and our national self-understanding; they have degraded the media and the entertainment industry, and subverted museums and other institutions entrusted with preserving the transmitting high culture. They have even, most poignantly, addled our hearts and innermost assumptions about what counts as the good life.

The initial source of the Sixties plague were the colleges and universities. Faculties and administrations surrendered instantly to student rampages and denunciations of traditional values, and many supposedly educational enterprises were, and remain, politicized.

That is why at the time William F. Buckley, Jr., said he would rather be governed by the first two thousand names in the Boston phone book than by the Harvard faculty. Now we are governed not by the Harvard faculty but by a pair of Yale law graduates with Sixties attitudes. I know what that means because both Bill and Hillary were my students when I taught at Yale. Well, I no longer say they were my students. I say they were in the room while I was teaching.

I recall, for example, I was a young associate professor, having just come to Yale, when the election of 1964 between Barry Goldwater and Lyndon Johnson was upon us. And one day there showed up in my office two young men from the *Yale Daily News*, the campus paper. They said they were looking for two professors to write columns on behalf of Lyndon Johnson and two to write columns on behalf of Barry Goldwater. They said they had hundreds clamoring to write the two columns for Lyndon Johnson, but so far, in a faculty of 2,000, they could only find one who was willing to write a column for Barry Goldwater. And they said that they had reason to suspect I might be the second.

Well, I did the principled thing, I said, go away. I haven't got tenure. Surely, you can find one other in a faculty of 2,000. And they went away sympathetic to my views on this matter and my situation. About three days later they came back. They said, we can't find a second one, and if you don't do it, Yale is going to look very silly with only one professor willing to endorse Barry Goldwater.

Well, I gave in, ill advisedly, and wrote the column, and the place exploded around me. They knew they wanted to hire one conservative, but they didn't think I really meant it. And all day long, every day, there was a stream of students and faculty coming in and out of my office arguing with me about this, and, very often, the last thing the person said upon leaving was "you must be crazy."

The election came and went, and I was sitting in my office when these two young men from the *Yale Daily News* showed up again. I can't tell you how delighted I was to see them. They said, we want to take you to lunch to meet the other Goldwater supporter. I went to lunch and met him, and he was crazy. But that was the current state of Yale then, and it's pretty much the state of Yale today.

And Yale is by no means unique. Look at almost any major college. The last holdout, the University of Chicago, is now going the way, slowly, of the other colleges. If I had to pick one significant item to prove it, it would be that the commencement speaker this year was Bill Clinton. That's the current state of Chicago and other schools.

We have these studies: Women's Studies, Black Studies, Hispanic Studies, Gay and Lesbian Studies, and during the time I taught at Yale, I noticed that every year the writing skills got worse and worse. It was not just writing, because if you can't write moderately clearly, the indication is that you can't think. And I think that is because even at the high school level, many schools have devalued education and returned to indoctrination so the students have attitudes rather than the ability to analyze.

With the decline in civic virtue and politicization of the universities, necessarily came a weakening of Americans' attachments to legitimate governmental processes, and with that self-restraint, which values the preservation of democratic procedures over immediate gratification of one's desires. The Founders would have been horrified, I believe, in the degree to which we, or many of us, have sacrificed self-government to self-seeking.

Increasingly, courts and uncontrolled bureaucracies make our moral choices for us, and we have little or no recourse. That this is no accidental phenomenon, not one that we suffer, for example, because of some bad luck in judicial appointments, is suggested by the fact that the same thing is happening all over the world where courts have complete independence from democratic will. Israel had managed to have the world's most activist Supreme Court, one that regularly sets aside the choices of the legislature, and their Court manages that without even having a constitution to cite.

One reason for this is the growth everywhere of intellectual classes, which, for reasons by now fairly well known, are left of center and tend to hold the desires of common people, and hence democracy, in some contempt. Many judges respond, often unconsciously, to the praise or criticism of those who control their reputations—law school and university faculties, print and electronic journalists, and intellectuals generally. Thus there are many rewards for moving to the cultural left, which our courts have been doing for over half a century, but few for adhering to the traditional standards of legal interpretation, and there is only grief for moving to the right. There have been many examples of justices moving to the left once they were on the Court but none of a justice moving to the right.

There was a professor of psychology who was teaching his class about conditioning people unconsciously to do what you want. After he had lectured for two hours the class grew weary and they decided to try it on him. He was a pacer. And as he paced towards the outside wall they paid rapt attention, took notes, just couldn't take their eyes off of him, and as he paced the other way, they began to rustle papers, sneak looks at the newspaper, and whisper to each other. Within 10 minutes they had him pinned to the outside wall. And I think that's what takes place in response to the intellectual elite class.

Simultaneously, we have witnessed the growth of the nanny state with the expansion of federal bureaucracies to serve every desire some group has been promised by politicians seeking election. Our politics have moved in this direction and to the left ever since the New Deal. The Founders tried to guard against the appearance of an all-powerful national government by enumerating the powers of Congress and adopting the Tenth Amendment, which states: "The powers not delegated to the United States by the Constitution, nor prohibited by it to the States, are reserved to the States respectively, or to the people."

That is a noble sentiment, and it is a dead letter.

As Edward Banfield pointed out, there is no way the national government could be confined to specific powers, and the very men who wrote the amendment began to violate it. The first to do so was George Washington. Other presidents followed. Today, I would not care to be the messenger who told the American people that programs such as Social Security, Medicare, Medicaid, as well as the labor and civil rights laws are outside the enumerated powers and are henceforward void.

Yet it is essential to individual liberty that government be smaller and less powerful than it is today. The only way to accomplish that is not be reciting some grand principles but by fighting program by program to shrink federal power as was done with welfare reform. That is not easy but it is the only realistic course.

One of the virtues of shrinking federal programs will be to end the struggle of groups for special privileges, all too often along ethnic and racial lines. We have to recognize that the United States is fracturing into separate tribes with the spread of such notions as diversity and multiculturalism. That process is all the harder to combat due to the massive flows of immigration, both legal and illegal.

In stressing diversity and multiculturalism, we tend to forget the historical importance to this nation of a single, unifying culture. In the second of *The Federalist Papers*, John Jay wrote that "Providence has been pleased to give this one connected country, to one united people, a people descended from the same ancestors, speaking the same language, professing the same religion, attached to the same principles of government, very similar in their manners and customs . . . . This country and this people seem to have made for each other . . . a band of brethren, united to each other by the strongest ties . . . ."

Few words could state more strongly the crucial importance of a common culture.

Since then we have had waves of immigration, which, while enriching our culture, blended into it. The public schools were a major agent for assimilation, viewing their task as making Americans out of Germans, Irish, Italians, and Russian Jews. Today, however, the public schools have been overcome by political correctness and cultural relativism, agents for fracturing our culture.

I most certainly do not want to leave you with the message that all is lost. Were they to return to America today, the Founders would not have found everything a cause for dismay. They would have been astounded and most of them pleased, for example, by the incredible wealth capitalism has produced in America. There are other nations with national resources as great or greater than our, but they have no free market to transform those resources into our standard of living. The free market, moreover, is important not merely for itself but as a force for political liberty and a symbol for personal freedom in non-market contexts. It is arguably the single greatest accomplishment of the United States and it stands as an example to the world, much of which is striving to emulate it.

Our forbears would be delighted too at the unbelievable inventiveness of Americans, an inventiveness that has produced successive revolutions in our way of life and that now, with the information age upon us, promises wealth, achievements, and freedom undreamed of not only in 1787, but in 1970. Benjamin Franklin would be ecstatic that his experiments with his kite and lightening have come so incredibly far. Whether we use our affluence wisely or foolishly remains to be seen, but that we are rich is good and a testament to continuing American dynamism.

However diluted, moreover, the democratic order that the Founders planned has survived remarkably intact after more than two centuries. We do not sufficiently realize what a jewel it is. The structure of the three branches as set out in the Constitution remains pretty much in working order. If the Bill of Rights has been distorted to protect things such as pornography and abortion, it also protects, as it was intended to, such freedoms as speech. This is no small accomplishment, to have planned a government and a document with such foresight that they continue as the framework of our nation today.

Having expressed some concerns about religion, culture, and politics in America today, I should note that there are, for the first time in some years, discernible and strong countertrends.

We should remember that there never has been a time in America when the Founders would have found a country entirely as they wished. George Washington, James Madison, Thomas Jefferson, John Adams, and the men who gathered at the Philadelphia Convention and debated in the ratifying conventions would surely have been appalled at the vulgarity and corruption of the era of Jacksonian popular democracy, they would have sorrowed over the divisions that led to the carnage of the Civil War and the sectional animosities that only in recent years have begun to subside, they would have disliked intensely the authoritarian nanny state that began with Franklin Roosevelt.

But the Founders would also have seen that America surmounted most of its difficulties, that it abolished the scourge of slavery and segregation. They would see that although it has a considerable distance yet to travel, America increasingly approximates the ideals of the Declaration of Independence.

The struggles ahead are to restore a common and decent culture, to relearn civic virtue, and to limit the reach of government at all levels. These are formidable tasks and victory is by no means assured.

A cause for hope is an intelligent, even intellectual, conservative movement, a relatively recent arrival upon the scene. In the mid-twentieth century, Lionel Trilling could say, with much truth, that there were no conservative ideas, merely irritable gestures. Today, we have conservative ideas of considerable depth and power—plus irritable gestures.

We have witnessed in our lifetimes the appearance of a wealth of conservative books, magazines, radio talk shows, columnists, and, by no means least, conservative think tanks that develop the ideas that can change minds and that conservative politicians can use. These are essential disseminators of news and ideas to break through the liberal, one-party media. Ronald Reagan credited the conservative generators of fresh thinking as influences on his policies and in making possible the coalition that led to his elections.

There are no Ronald Reagans to be seen in our politics today and chances are there will never be another, but that means instead of waiting for a savior, we will have to work harder to achieve our own and America's salvation. People sometimes accuse me of being a pessimist, but when I am in company like this, I can't help optimism bubbling to the surface.

A keen observer once said that God takes special care of drunks and the United States of America. But with the help of organizations like The Heritage Foundation, and, if I may say so, the American Enterprise Institute, perhaps we won't have to rely entirely on Divine Providence.

ABOUT THE AUTHORS

Robert H. Bork is a Senior Fellow at the American Enterprise Institute. He has served as a circuit court judge, lawyer, educator, and acting Attorney General of the United States. He was nominated by President Ronald Reagan to the position of Associate Justice of the Supreme Court of the United States in 1987, but his confirmation was denied by the Senate. Judge Bork is the author of several books, including *Slouching Towards Gomorrah: Modern Liberalism and American Decline* (1996) and *The Tempting of America: The Political Seduction of the Law* (1990).

Edwin J. Feulner is President of The Heritage Foundation. He is also Senior Vice President and Trustee of the Mont Pelerin Society, member of the Board of Visitors of George Mason University, and a trustee of Regis University, the Acton Institute, the Council for National Policy, and the International Republican Institute. Dr. Feulner is the author of several books, including *The March of Freedom* (1998), *Conservatives Stalk the House* (1983), and *Looking Back* (1981). His syndicated column appears in more than 500 newspapers.

Kim R. Holmes is Vice President of The Heritage Foundation and Director of its Kathryn and Shelby Cullom Davis Institute for International Studies. Before joining Heritage, he was a Senior Fellow at the Institute for Foreign Policy Analysis. Dr. Holmes is the co-editor of *Restoring American Leadership: A U.S. Foreign and Defense Policy Blueprint* and *The Index of Economic Freedom.*

Charles R. Kesler is Director of the Henry Salvatori Center for the Study of Individual Freedom in the Modern World and Associate Professor of Government at Claremont McKenna College. He is a Senior Fellow at, and sits on the board of, the Claremont Institute for the Study of Statesmanship and Political Philosophy. Dr. Kesler is the editor of the Penguin–Putnam edition of *The Federalist Papers*; *Saving the Revolution: The Federalist Papers and the American Founding*; and, with William F. Buckley Jr., *Keeping the Tablets: Modern American Conservative Thought.*

Michael Novak is the George Fredrick Jewett Chair in Religion, Philosophy and Public Policy and Director of Social and Political Studies at the American Enterprise Institute. He received the Templeton Prize for Progress in Religion in 1994 and the Boyer Award in 1999. Mr. Novak has written 25 influential books concerning the philosophy and theology of culture, including *The Catholic Ethic and the Spirit of Capitalism* (1993), *Business as a Calling* (1996), and *The Fire of Invention* (1997), and was co-founder of *The World*, *Crisis*, and *First Things* magazines.

Matthew Spalding is Director of the B. Kenneth Simon Center for American Studies and Director of Lectures and Educational Programs at The Heritage Foundation. He is an Adjunct Fellow at the Claremont Institute and a member of the Board of Academic Advisors at Mount Vernon Estate. Dr. Spalding is the co-author of *A Sacred Union of Citizens: Washington's Farewell Address and the American Character* and the editor of *Patriot Sage: George Washington and the American Political Tradition.*

Malcolm Wallop is the Chairman of Frontiers of Freedom, a nonprofit organization he established in January 1995 to study and research issues pertaining to limited government and constitutional freedoms, and a Senior Fellow at The Heritage Foundation. He was elected to the United States Senate and served three terms beginning in 1976; he served on numerous committees, including Energy and Natural Resources, Finance, Small Business, Armed Services, and the Select Committee on Intelligence. Senator Wallop is the co-author of *The Arms Control Delusion*.

Walter E. Williams is the John M. Olin Distinguished Professor of Economics and Chairman of the Economics Department at George Mason University. He serves on the boards of directors of several organizations, including Citizens for a Sound Economy, the Reason Foundation, and the Hoover Institution. Dr. Williams has authored several books, including *Do the Right Think: The People's Economist Speaks* and *More Liberty Means Less Government*.